THE GREEN WITCH'S HERB AND PLANT ENCYCLOPEDIA

THE GREEN WITCH'S HERB AND PLANT ENCYCLOPEDIA

150 Ingredients for Everyday Witchcraft

ROWAN MORGANA

callisto
publishing
an imprint of Sourcebooks

TO GAIA

CONTENTS

—————————— PART I ——————————

GROWING A MAGICAL PRACTICE 1

—————————— PART II ——————————

MAGICAL PLANT PROFILES 49

Blessed Thistle 68	Daffodil 92	Honesty 116
Blueberry 69	Dandelion 93	Honeysuckle 117
Borage 70	Datura 94	Horehound 118
Bracken 71	Dill 95	Horsetail 119
Bromeliad 72	Dock 96	Hydrangea 120
Broom 73	Dogwood 97	Ivy 121
Burdock 74	Echinacea 98	Jasmine 122
Buttercup 75	Elder 99	Juniper 123
Caraway 76	Fennel 100	Lady's Mantle 124
Carnation 77	Feverfew 101	Lavender 125
Catnip 78	Flax 102	Lemon Balm 126
Cedar 79	Foxglove 103	Lilac 127
Chamomile 80	Galangal 104	Lily 128
Chicory 81	Gardenia 105	Lovage 129
Chickweed 82	Garlic 106	Magnolia 130
Chile Pepper 83	Goldenrod 107	Maidenhair Fern 131
Chrysanthemum 84	Grape 108	Mallow 132
Cinnamon 85	Hawthorn 109	Mandrake 133
Cinquefoil 86	Hazel 110	Marigold 134
Clover 87	Heather 111	Marjoram 135
Columbine 88	Heliotrope 112	Meadowsweet 136
Comfrey 89	Hellebore 113	Mint 137
Cowslip 90	Henbane 114	Mistletoe 138
Cyclamen 91	Holly 115	Moringa 139

INTRODUCTION

The *Green Witch's Herb and Plant Encyclopedia* will help you open your heart to the rhythms of Mother Earth and the natural world. Inside you'll find a profile of 150 herbs and plants to incorporate into your magical practice, plus a primer on gardening and some spells to get you started.

It's incredibly satisfying to grow and harvest your own plants for your magical practice, but you don't have to be a gardener to use and enjoy this book. Dried herbs and flowers are readily available and are an easy and convenient way to begin working with plants. I grow most of the herbs and flowers that I need, and what I don't produce, I can forage from the nearby forests, fields, and rivers. If you're fortunate to live in or have access to a rural area, you'll be able to pick and choose from a bounty of wild herbs and flowers that you can easily collect.

If you're a city dweller and don't have access to an outdoor space, you can grow potted plants on a patio or deck or near a bright, sunny window; also, there are parks and open spaces where you can forage for many excellent herbal resources. Enhance and uphold your plants' attributes (healing, happiness, banishing, etc.) with your intention as they grow by using the technique of visualization, which is simply "seeing in your mind what you want to happen." Many plants suitable for Green Witch magic do very well indoors.

I hope that everyone interested in working with and attuning to the energies of the plant world and Green Witchcraft will find inspiration from this book and the confidence to unearth the powers of natural magic.

HOW TO USE THIS BOOK

The *Green Witch's Herb and Plant Encyclopedia* will help you begin your herbal path with confidence. You'll discover how to live with the rhythms of the Earth as you grow and use the natural energy of plants to create healing, balance, and harmony in your life.

In part 1, the lore, customs, beliefs, and training of a Green Witch will empower you with the practical aspects of Green Witchcraft. You'll discover how to plant, harvest, nurture, and use plants, and you'll connect with a patron spirit or two who will guide you on your sacred path. We will touch on creating a green sanctuary where you may attune to the spirits of the Earth and learn basic magic skills like grounding, visualization, creating sacred space, and intention setting. In chapter 3, you'll put your knowledge into practice and begin casting spells and doing rituals that have been created especially for the Green Witch.

In part 2, you can explore the 150 plants most used in Green Witch magic. The profiles include a quick reference box with tips and details about growing, caring for, and using each plant magically. Some plants are more suitable for foraging; those plants include sourcing location. Remember to rely on foraging guides for plant identification and safe usage. When you mindfully consume a plant to create a magical change, your body automatically connects to its spiritual attributes; the plant energy upholds and aligns with your intention. Before consuming any part of the edible or nontoxic plants listed in part 2, do further research, as there is great variance within genera. Part 2 also includes classic poison herbs of witchcraft and many traditional herbs that every witch should know.

PART I
✠✠✠✠✠✠✠

GROWING A MAGICAL PRACTICE

CHAPTER ONE

GREEN WITCHCRAFT AND THE MAGIC OF PLANTS

Plants are living spirits with their own unique identities that are rooted in the deep knowledge of Mother Earth. We have depended on them throughout the ages for food, medicine, clothing, art, building material, and magic. Our lives and the plant world are intricately entwined, weaving a tapestry of beliefs, customs, and inspiration. We can harness their power as our botanical allies for protection, health, love, and nearly every other purpose under the sun, moon, and stars. Sit beside a plant with an open heart and mind for a while, and you'll appreciate how deeply connected you are to the natural world.

✦ A Brief History of Plants, Magic, and Green Witchcraft

Green Witchcraft is a spiritual path profoundly linked with Earth energy and channeling nature's power through magic, healing, and life choices. The soul of a Green Witch entwines with the seasonal cycles of Mother Earth as plants sprout, grow, mature, and are harvested. The Elemental energies—Earth as soil, Air as wind, Fire as the sun, and the life-giving Water Element—combine with the simplicity of common everyday items like feathers or stones to create the basis of Green Witch magic. When the land spirits whisper on the morning breeze, the Green Witch listens, and when night falls, the spell of darkness is embraced without fear or hesitation, for the Green Witch knows that the duality of light and dark is necessary to achieve balance. The potions, brews, spells, and worship created from available resources shadow the path of the ancestors from thousands of years ago.

THE TENETS OF GREEN WITCHCRAFT

The Green Witch is a healer, nurturer, and protector who works with the energy of the Earth Mother. There is no dogma, higher authority, or formal tradition with degree systems and initiation. According to their core beliefs, the Green Witch follows a personal code of conduct. Though there are no written rules, there are commonalities that most would agree upon:

1. Love of plants and gardens
2. Respect for nature and all things wild and free
3. Uses natural found objects in magic
4. Uses natural sources for magic power
5. Works with nature spirits
6. Is mindful of their impact on nature
7. Uses plants as primary spell and ritual ingredients
8. Is a healer and nurturer
9. Actively protects and honors the Earth
10. Aligns with the natural rhythms of the Earth
11. Lives a healthy, sustainable lifestyle

THE GREEN WITCHCRAFT TRADITION

The tradition of Green Witchcraft doesn't have a set of ethical codes to be followed, nor do most Green Witches consider their practice a religion with specific holy days, rules, deities, and particular ways of doing things. Of course, you're free to observe all the seasonal celebrations honored by other faiths; it's entirely your choice. If you're not into any recognized holidays, you can always observe the changing seasons, from spring to summer and fall to winter, which are the plant world's guideposts for sowing, tending, reaping, and rest. Walking the path of Green Witch is a way of life, a spiritual journey of the soul that embraces the Earth as a living, breathing entity.

Green Witchcraft stems from the folk magic of long ago, from the healers, village wise women, and cunning folk who understood the healing and magic abilities of the plants around them. They knew how to use them in their potions, spells, and philters to achieve a desired magical outcome, and they shared their knowledge through word of mouth or hands-on training of an assistant or acolyte.

There are no formal instructions specific to Green Witchcraft, but there are several excellent books on the market, and there's a lot of free information on the internet. (See Resources, page 207.). You can undoubtedly educate yourself by studying books on botany, gardening, pagan plant correspondences, herbal healing, and magic. Though there isn't an official degree or initiation system for Green Witchcraft, you may want to mark your decision to become a Green Witch by having your own Green Witch Dedication Ritual found in chapter 3.

To practice Green Witchcraft, you'll have to get your hands dirty! Create a garden, plant some seeds, and buy some houseplants! Bring out your mortar and pestle and tend your simmering cauldron of herbs while you lovingly create a healing potion. Have an autumn kitchen filled with the aroma of drying flowers and an overflowing apothecary of jars and bottles filled with plants, flowers, herbs, and spices. Grab your kitchen shears and your watering can, go and harvest what's ripe, and bless what's growing. Walk barefoot in the soil and revel in the feelings of freedom and peace that your garden will provide you.

Walking the path of a Green Witch means maintaining inner balance and alignment with your principles and beliefs so that you may grow into your authentic self. A Green Witch knows that with the passing of daylight into darkness, there is always a shadow side that must be acknowledged, addressed, and brought into the light of understanding.

SAFETY AND TOXICITY

Not all plants are safe to handle; identify them correctly before working with any herb. Some plants are completely benign, whereas others are dangerous to touch or inhale. Every plant in this book is clearly marked as *toxic, nontoxic,* or *poisonous.*

The toxic and poisonous plants should not be ingested and must be handled with care; the poisonous plants should not be touched unless you're wearing gloves. The difference between toxic and poisonous in this book is that toxic plants can make you very ill but probably won't kill you; the poisonous plants can cause death. Toxicity to pets is included in the plant profiles to protect your fur babies.

If you are pregnant or nursing, be very careful when working with herbs; never ingest them, and wear gloves whenever possible when handling plants.

Once you understand common herbs' safety factors, you can choose which ones you want to grow. When you start your plants from seed or bring them home from the nursery, you can infuse them with power by informing them of their magical potential whenever you work with them. Got a pot of marigolds? Tell them that they are pure sun power and filled with protection. If you have a sickly plant, place an amethyst or rose quartz crystal empowered with healing energy near the plant's roots as you envision health and vitality. Treat your plants with respect and reverence to increase their transcendent qualities. Mass-produced packages of dried herbs won't have the potency of ones you grow yourself! Care for your plants with love, shower them with positive energy, and soon you'll have a garden filled with powerful magical allies.

THE GREEN WITCH'S HERB AND PLANT ENCYCLOPEDIA

✦ Herbs and Plants in Practice

We are surrounded by plants every single day of our lives, but how often do we stop to really appreciate the beauty of the green world? We buy packaged spices at the grocery store to use in cooking without considering the mysterious powers that even the most ordinary herbs possess. Every herb you have in your spice cabinet contains magic! Cinnamon can boost power when added to any spell, cloves protect you and drive away negative energy, and ginger can bring you money and love. Your flower garden, filled with color and scent, can entice fairies, butterflies, and bees to make their homes there, and even your everyday houseplants can become a handy source for healing balms and herbal sachets. Create an outdoor shrine to the spirits of the land or dedicate an indoor flowerpot as a Green Witch Altar; see Foxglove Fairy Altar (page 40).

What makes a plant magical? Since the beginning of time, humans and plants have had a symbiotic relationship. Plants have fed us, healed us, enhanced our spiritual lives, and gifted us with unbelievable beauty. We inhale one another's breaths throughout our lives and compost together into Mother Earth when our cycle is over. We have studied plants and have extensive written records filled with information on their cultivation, preservation, cooking, healing, magic, and spiritual attributes. Basil (page 58), a kitchen staple, can bring you luck. Yarrow (page 198), a roadside weed, can open your mind to psychic experiences. Unlock the secrets of the plants and flowers that are all around you.

✦ Powers of Plants

Plants are living, breathing entities that are affected by light, heat, food, water, soil, and your mood or intention when you're near them. Plant lore is rich in history, healing, and magic, and along the way, most plants have acquired several names, which can be confusing.

Common or folk name: What the local people called it; plants can have several similar common names

Botanical name: The exact Latin name for individual plants; an accurate way to identify a plant

Magical name: The arcane naming system of magical plants

GREAT STARTS FOR GREEN WITCHES

PLANT/HERB	MAGICAL USES
AGRIMONY	• hex-breaking • protection • sleep
WORMWOOD	• astral travel • binding • clairvoyance
BASIL	• brings good luck • heals quarrels • invites wealth
BAY	• brings protection • increases clairvoyance • promotes healing
CHIVES	• banishes depression • protects from illness
MULLEIN	• promotes courage • used in defensive magic • banishes baneful energy
HAWTHORN	• aids fertility • sacred to fairies • happiness
HONEYSUCKLE	• enhances love • inspires generosity • promotes peace
HYSSOP	• purifies sacred space • banishes evil spells • clears negative energy
JUNIPER	• anti-theft • health • purifies and protects

PLANT/HERB	MAGICAL USES
LAVENDER	• induces sleep • invites peace • promotes love and joy
MANDRAKE	• fertility • protection • spirit world
MORINGA	• increases courage • health • strength
MUGWORT	• banishes baneful spirits • messages • enhances divination
ROSEMARY	• increases memory • alleviates sorrow • used in past-life magic
SAGE	• used in ritual cleansing • promotes mental health • used for consecration
THYME	• attracts garden fairies • new moon magic • used in ritual bathing
VALERIAN	• induces calmness • brings sleep • used in love spells
VERVAIN	• used to bless altars • promotes peace • useful in most magic
YARROW	• promotes courage • exorcism • boosts psychic powers

The plant profiles will list the botanical and common plant names along with the following magic correspondences:

GENDER

Plant gender has nothing to do with being either male or female; instead, it's a way of describing the plant's vibration. Masculine plants, such as pepper and tobacco, are robust, stimulating, and aggressive, whereas feminine plants, like rose and lemon balm, are relaxing, passive, and subtle. Masculine plants are ruled by the Elements of Air and Fire and are used in forceful magic, like overcoming, strengthening, breaking, and removing. Feminine plants are governed by the Elements of Water and Earth and are used in attraction magic, like love, emotions, healing, and spirituality.

PLANETARY RULER

Plants have a planetary ruler chosen from the seven traditional celestial bodies known to the ancient astrologers. The planetary influence will expand your working knowledge of their magical uses by adding another layer of attributes for you to draw upon.

Sun: God mysteries, protection, strength, power, purification

Moon: Goddess mysteries, dreams, intuition, spiritual growth

Mars: Competitions, conflicts, courage, war

Mercury: Communication, divination, self-improvement

Jupiter: Dedication, endurance, luck, money

Venus: Art, fertility, music, pleasure, love

Saturn: Banishing, responsibility, determination, rules

ELEMENTAL RULER

Plants fall into one of the four Elemental categories. The Elements are considered the building blocks of all creation and the foundation of magic.

Earth: North, darkness, end of cycles, spirit world, green

Air: East, dawn, new beginnings, movement, intellect, yellow

CHAPTER TWO

THE GREEN WITCH'S MAGICAL GARDEN

This chapter will explore indoor and outdoor gardening with practical information on caring for your plants, including tips on cultivation, basic gardening, watering, pruning, weeding, and fertilizing. There's also a section on the basics of wild foraging to help you obtain plants you can't or don't grow yourself. A big part of the craft of the Green Witch is preserving and storing plants for future use. You'll learn what you need to know about storage techniques like drying, freezing, and refrigerating. I'll also explain grounding and why your garden is the perfect place to practice it.

✦ Establishing a Green Space in Your Home

If you're not interested in establishing a garden outdoors, you can still find the space indoors to practice Green Witchcraft. Decide the energies you want to bring into your home, and then, using the plant profiles in this book, choose which houseplants will work best for you! Your indoor plants can support your journey into the natural world of earth power just as easily as an outdoor garden. Plants are all around us; they're readily available in your local grocery store and at florists, and there are garden centers filled with a huge variety of herbal allies just waiting for you to bring them home. Go for a walk and collect twigs and leaves, discover their inner magic, and use them in your spells! Fill your kitchen with jars of dried herbs and go to your local farmers' market to add to your herbal arsenal. Buy a bouquet of flowers and enjoy them while they're fresh; then dry and preserve them for future use.

✦ Essential Equipment for Magical Gardening

Now that you understand what the Green Witch is and does, it's time to think about some of the extras you may want to purchase besides your standard hand trowel and gardening gloves. Choose whatever resonates with you and aligns with how you want to practice your craft. Add some traditional herbal magic equipment, and you'll be ready to connect with the power of the green world. If you're going to grow, harvest, and preserve your plants, you'll need some tools. Be sure to have separate, designated, labeled tools if you work with poisonous plants.

Garden journal. To record everything about your plants and garden; consider it your plant Book of Shadows.

Jars and bottles. For storing dried herbs, spells, powders, and liquids. Don't forget the labels!

Mortar and pestle. To grind plants for potions, philters, sachets, and powders. Use a heavy stone mortar for tough herbs and a wooden one for delicate plants.

Dehydrator. Plants can be successfully air-dried if they have a low moisture content, but using a dehydrator dramatically improves their overall quality.

Cutting tools. Use scissors to harvest and prune delicate herbs, or you can use a dedicated ritual knife for magical harvesting. You'll need a pair of pruning shears for larger, tougher plants.

✦ Indoor Gardening

If you have little or no outdoor gardening space, indoor container gardening is for you! Indoor gardening can be therapeutic, and some people find that plants are company for them. Many people believe that talking or playing music to plants makes the plants happy and helps them thrive! Indoor growing offers protection from harsh weather conditions, and you can tailor how much light your plants receive by situating them closer to or farther from windows and controlling how much sun comes through the glass. You can also supplement the light source by using grow lights. Your indoor plants are not as susceptible to insects and pests; though harmful bugs can still attack, it's much easier to control or stop an infestation indoors. Having a few pots of indoor plants is relatively inexpensive compared to outdoor gardening; you really don't need much more than plants, suitable plant pots, a watering can, and some knowledge about your plants' requirements.

You can create a plant shrine or altar by adding statues of deities or patrons, crystals, or other sacred objects to your plant pot. Write petitions or prayers on ribbons and attach them to branches or paint sigils, images, words, or incantations—outside or inside the container! Add the energy of the Sun and Moon to your plants by giving them Sun Water (water placed in the Sun for a day to promote energy and vitality) or with Moon Water (water left overnight in the Full Moonlight to bestow the powers of intuition and magic).

Allowing children to help you tend your plants teaches them the responsibility and routine of caring for a living thing. If you love the look of big, lush pots of plants in your living space and want your home to feel inviting and calming, go ahead and bring the outdoors inside with indoor gardening.

Fill your home or sacred space with beautiful and magical plants. See part 2, Magical Plant Profiles (page 49). All plants are holy, but you can make them even more so by whispering encouraging prayers, charging the soil with crystals or with the energy of your hands, and sitting with the plant in meditation. If your plant is edible, you may want to make a tea or sprinkle its leaves on food to help you consciously bond with it and receive its healing and wisdom. To honor the Elements (see plant profiles), put your plants in their appropriate direction, such as Water-ruled aloe in the West and Fire-ruled ginger in the South.

✦ Outdoor Gardening

Not everyone has access to outdoor garden space, but if you're lucky enough to have a plot of land, you'll be able to expand your plant-growing experience. Outdoor gardening is a bit more complicated than indoor growing because everything's on a bigger scale and needs more physical effort, but the benefits are well worth it! You can still use containers outdoors; they're the easiest way to begin. When plants are in pots, they're higher off the ground, so working with them is more manageable, especially for older people or people with physical disabilities.

Raised-bed gardens sit on top of the ground and have a border around them to contain the soil. You'll have to build the walls and purchase the soil, so they can be a bit pricey. Raised beds can be anywhere from a few inches to a few feet deep, and they're a great choice if you need to save space or if you don't have a lot of time for weeding and watering, but they can also dry out faster than an in-ground garden. Raised-bed crops are grown closer together, producing a higher yield per square foot, but certain plants won't do well in a raised bed. Plants that take up a lot of room, like pumpkins, watermelon, and corn, are happier if planted in the ground.

In-ground gardens need heavy-duty gardening tools, like a wheelbarrow, shovel, rake, and hoe, but they are the least expensive way to grow plants in the long run. The advantages of this type of garden are that you can use the existing soil (though you may need to add amendments) and grow virtually any crop (if it can thrive where you live), and your garden can be as big as your outdoor space permits.

CULTIVATING MAGICAL PLANTS

As a Green Witch, you'll want to grow as many plants as possible for your magical practice. Plants you've interacted with daily become infused with your energy and spirit. They know you! Your homegrown plants bond to your energetic profile and are more powerful magically than commercially grown plants, which have been raised and harvested inside an industry and have witnessed many unknown energies. Of course, you probably won't be able to grow and preserve every plant you want or need, and you'll inevitably have to buy them already processed. You can get lots of dried herbs and spices from the grocery or local health food store and order them online; that's okay, but be aware that they won't be as strong for spells, rituals, or healing. Purchased plant materials should be cleansed of negative energy and reenergized by charging them with your intention (see page 32).

✦ Basic Garden Care

Creating and maintaining your garden will require some thought, care, and attention. The first thing to do is find the perfect location! You'll want your garden to receive at least six hours of sunlight a day and be close to a water source like an outdoor tap. Before planting, research plants that grow well in your location, what to feed them, and how much light and water they need. Knowing your area's frost and planting dates is a good idea for successful planting. This information is readily available online from the *Farmers' Almanac*.

WATERING

The right amount of water is essential to your plant's growth and health. A rule of thumb is to water your plants early in the morning when the top inch of soil is almost dry. Plants in direct sunlight need more water than shaded plants, and potted plants may need watering more than once a day. Some plants are drought tolerant, whereas others are very thirsty. Find out the water requirements for each plant to create a regular watering schedule.

Plants need water to remain erect, convert the Sun's energy into food, and move nutrients from their roots to their leaves. Using too much water can be just as damaging as too little. If your plants aren't thriving, the first thing to look at is how much water you give them. Signs of overwatering are yellowing or black leaves, wilting when the soil is wet, and mildew. Signs of underwatering are wilting; dry, brown leaf tips; and stunted growth. If you're experiencing any of these problems, test the soil around your plants. Dig down about 6 inches near the roots; your plants don't need water if the soil is moist. If it's dry, give the plants some water, wait an hour, and then do the digging test again. Potted plants and hanging baskets will dry out quickly on hot, windy summer days; test the moisture content before watering by poking your finger into the soil. If it's still moist, don't water it! Potted mint and parsley prefer to be consistently moist; potted thyme and rosemary prefer to dry out between waterings.

PRUNING, PINCHING, AND DEADHEADING

Prune to shape your plant and remove dead leaves or branches. The best time to prune is usually the winter or early spring, but you can remove dead and diseased branches at any time. Pinch your plants when they're actively growing to encourage bushy growth. To pinch your plant, remove the very top of the plant stem above dormant leaf nodes (they look like two bumps on either side of the stem); the nodes will produce two new branches. You can harvest parts of your plant anytime by pinching or pruning, but before gathering any part of the plant, ask for permission. Be respectful of your plant allies, listen intuitively for a clear "yes," and be sure to show your gratitude by giving an offering, such as pure water, a bit of compost, or a simple prayer of thanks.

Deadhead your plants by cutting off faded or dead blossoms to encourage flowering and prevent your plant from going to seed. If you'd like to save some seeds, take off all but a few of the dead flowers. Deadheaded flowers can be kept for use in floral wreaths or as natural confetti, added to potpourris, or offered to land or nature spirits.

WEEDING

Whenever you grow plants, you'll have weeds. Any plant that's growing where it's competing with a cultivated plant for food, water, and space can be called a weed. Weeding your garden can be a very meditative and grounding experience, especially if you're confident you're doing it correctly. Here are some weeding tips:

- Weed when the soil is damp; pulling out the plants is much easier. Be sure to get all the roots.

- Mulch your garden, and don't leave any bare earth for weeds to grow in.

- Dispose of weeds by putting them in the garbage (check municipal regulations first), composting them, or burning them.

- Use the proper tools:

  - A three-pronged cultivator is great for small areas and getting in close to plant stems.

  - A long-handled garden hoe is best for removing shallow-rooted weeds in larger areas.

  - A V-notched weeder works for plants with long taproots.

FERTILIZING

Your plants will regularly need fertilizer to help them grow healthy and strong. Fertilizers are concentrated nutrients that consist of three main ingredients:

Nitrogen creates green leafy plants and helps with photosynthesis.

Phosphorous stimulates healthy root growth and is necessary for the development of buds and flowers.

Potassium promotes healthy, vigorous plants with more resistance to pests and disease.

Fertilizer can be purchased as dry granules or as a concentrated liquid. The quickest and easiest way to fertilize a large garden is by applying dry fertilizer around the base of your plants. Liquid fertilizers are diluted with water and poured around or directly onto the plant foliage and are the best way to fertilize containers or individual plants.

Organic fertilizer consists of natural ingredients like manure, seaweed, or compost. It is easy on your plants because it feeds them slowly over a more extended period. Organic fertilizer improves the soil and stimulates root growth. You can make organic fertilizer by steeping chopped comfrey, nettle, or horsetail in water for a few weeks and then straining the brew and using it like any liquid fertilizer.

Chemical fertilizers are affordable and work quickly, but they can burn your plants and, if overused, can create a toxic buildup in your soil.

If you're feeling stressed, distracted, or unbalanced, your garden and plants can bring you back to the center by reconnecting you to the Earth. Mindful grounding promotes balance and lowers stress levels. Another word for grounding is *earthing*, and that's precisely what it is: a physical connection to the Earth. The simplest form of grounding involves nothing more than walking barefoot in your garden or placing your hands directly on the ground. Try sitting with your back to a tree and absorbing its stable, rooted energy. Earthing techniques can deepen your sense of peace and are effective indoors or out.

The following grounding exercise is a classic earthing technique. Visualize your feet growing roots that extend deep into Mother Earth, and then imagine all your cares and worries flowing down the roots into the ground. Imagine Earth energy flowing up the roots and filling your body with stable, grounded energy.

✦ Harvesting

Increase the magical powers of your plants by practicing conscious harvesting with these guidelines:

- Inform the plant spirits of your intention.
- Ask permission before you cut.
- Don't take more than you need.
- Be open to the plant energy and any messages it has for you.
- Show gratitude and leave an offering.

Gather plant material by clipping top growth, flowers, stems, and branches during the growing season, but don't take more than 25 percent of the plant.

WHEN TO HARVEST

The optimum time to harvest your plants is when the dew has dried in the early morning. Many Green Witches plant and harvest according to the Moon phases; they gather aboveground crops during the Full Moon and belowground crops on the Dark or New Moon. A busy life may get in the way of an ideal harvesting time, so if the plant's ready before the correct Moon phase arrives, go ahead and harvest it! Pick flowers from buds to full-blown blossoms, cut herbs before they flower for optimum potency, harvest fruit and berries when fully ripe, and gather vegetables just before maturity. If you want to collect seeds, harvest the flowers once they have finished blooming and lost their petals, an then dry them on a paper towel.

HOW TO HARVEST

Harvesting with intention builds your relationship with plants and contributes to their power. Before doing anything, please spend a few moments connecting with the plant, looking it over, positively identifying it, and ensuring it's healthy. Ask the plant's permission before cutting it and explain why you want to harvest it. You'll receive a "yes" or "no" answer intuitively; listen to your gut feeling and respect a "no" response. When harvesting, focus on the reason you're gathering the plant. If it's for a spell, concentrate on the desired outcome. If it's for food, consider your gratitude. Once harvested, thank the plant for the sacrifice it's made, offer a silent prayer, and leave something in return, like water, compost, or a small crystal.

Herbs. Cut foliage herbs, like parsley, basil, oregano, and thyme, before flowering. Gather flowering herbs, like lavender and chamomile, as soon as the blossoms begin to open. Harvest seed herbs, like coriander and dill, once the seeds have dried on the plant. Clip off the seed heads and put them in a paper bag; then shake the bag to separate the seeds from the chaff.

Flowers. Cut flowers like roses and peonies in the morning and immediately plunge the stems in water if you're not drying them for storage. Harvest buds or partially opened or full-blown flowers anytime. If you're only after petals, clip off the flower head, gently pull the petals off, and dry them in a paper bag.

Roots. Harvest roots, like mandrake and belladonna, once they're two years old. Loosen the soil with a garden fork 8 inches from the base, and use your gloved hands to extract the root, taking care not to break or snap it.

Branches and twigs. Look for fallen branches on the ground before cutting if you're foraging in the wild. Cut branches cleanly near the base.

FORAGING

Foraging or wildcrafting is the art of harvesting wild plants. It's a beautiful way to be out in the natural world and connect with Mother Earth. It's a sustainable and cost-effective way to use plants that live and thrive where you do. Local plants include plants native to your area, naturalized plants that have established themselves as part of the environment, and plants that have been placed or grown in a garden or park. They are saturated with local energy and the spirits of the area and will more easily align with you and your purpose or intention. No matter where you live, you'll find a variety of plants that will be useful in your magical practice.

Before you begin foraging, know your plant! Use a field guide and have the plant's correct botanical name. Don't harvest or consume any plants you can't positively identify.

A basket or bags, scissors, and knives are the essential tools for wildcrafting. Wear protective clothing and gloves; you never know when you'll run into poison ivy or thorns. A long stick will help you move aside prickly underbrush and can be used to shake fruit or nuts from unreachable branches. You'll need a small hand trowel or digging fork if you're after roots.

Forage in season, meaning you will be collecting roots in the winter; young leaves and buds in the spring; leaves, blossoms, and fruit in the summer; and roots, seeds, and berries in autumn. The best time to harvest is in the morning just after the dew has dried; avoid harvesting in wet weather or the hot sun. Keep a record of when and where you harvested to make future foraging easier.

The quickest way to begin foraging is in your backyard, or you could ask neighbors or private landowners for permission to wildcraft on their land. Many landowners are amenable to foraging, so it won't hurt to ask! It's never okay to forage without permission. If you plan to gather from public land or state and national parks, be aware of the laws; calling or writing the regulatory office of the Bureau of Land Management may be necessary.

Some of the wealthiest resources of diverse plant life are at the edges and margins, where a forest opens onto a field or land meets water. The suburbs may also yield plenty of diversity, but beware of harvesting near homes or agricultural areas because of possible pesticide and herbicide use. Avoid roadsides, parking lots, and industrial areas. Don't collect from nature reserves, as these are areas set up to protect wild species. Be respectful and leave them untouched.

Follow foraging sustainability and etiquette:

- Don't harvest endangered or rare plants.

- Know what plants are invasive and how they spread.

- Only take what you need.

- Take care not to damage the plant.

- Don't pull plants out by the roots.

- Leave the foraging area clean and tidy.

- Don't forage with large groups.

- Don't take more than 10 percent of a patch of plants; leave some for others.

- Don't trample plants or make new trails.

You can find a local foraging group for your area at FindAForager.com, and there are plenty of YouTube videos on foraging. You can even download foraging apps for your phone and browse local foraging websites for lots of information. Don't use this book for foraging plant identification; instead, check out the Resources (page 207) at the back of this book.

✦ Drying and Preserving

Once you've harvested your plant material, you'll want to preserve it for future use. Drying is the most common and reliable method to store and keep fresh herbs, but freezing or placing the stems in water may be the best option depending on the plant. Flowers or plants that are a bit more delicate may need to be desiccated in silica gel. Once you have decided on the correct preservation method, you can choose a storage container and create some labels. Remember to label everything; trust me, you will forget what's in that bag or jar after a few weeks!

HERBS

The easiest method to dry herbs is to bundle them with twine and hang them to dry. Avoid direct sunlight and check the plants weekly. Plants are ready when the leaves crumble easily. It's a good idea to label the plant bundles; they all tend to look alike once they're dried. If you can't hang your plants to dry, you can put them on a drying rack out of direct sunlight.

If you need to preserve the whole plant or collect seeds, use a labeled paper bag; as the plants dry, the seeds will fall to the bottom of the bag. Check herbs after about a week and then daily until dry.

To oven-dry herbs, arrange them on a parchment paper–lined baking sheet and bake at 100°F for a few hours until they crumble easily.

A dehydrator is a fast and easy way to preserve your herbs. Place a single layer on the dehydrator trays and dry for 20 minutes to 4 hours.

Microwave dehydration works well for tender leaves like parsley and basil. Put the leaves between two paper towels and microwave on high for 30 seconds; continue until well dried.

A great way to preserve herbs is to freeze them. Chop the plant into usable pieces, freeze on a baking sheet, and store in a labeled freezer bag. You can also freeze chopped herbs in an ice cube tray. Put a tablespoon into each compartment, add water, freeze, and transfer the cubes to labeled freezer bags.

FLOWERS AND NONEDIBLE PLANTS

Flowers and nonedibles can also be bundled, air-dried, oven-dried, microwaved, and dehydrated. To preserve whole flowers, use silica gel. Put an inch of silica gel in the bottom of a microwavable container, add the flowers, and pour more gel over the blooms—microwave on low for 2 to 5 minutes. When done, remove the container, cover it, and let it sit for 24 hours before removing the flowers.

You can also dry hardy flowers by covering them with sand. When adding the sand, support the flower with a chopstick or a small paintbrush. Wait for 2 weeks, and if the flowers are completely dry, carefully remove them from the sand.

An old-fashioned way of preserving flowers is by pressing them in a book. Sandwich the flower between two pieces of parchment, close it in the center of a book, and pile some more heavy books on top. The flowers will be ready after 2 to 4 weeks.

The safest way to dry toxic or poisonous plants, like belladonna or aconite, is by hanging them to dry in a paper bag in an out-of-the-way place that pets and children can't access. Label the bag! Draw skull and crossbones! Be careful! Once dried, toxic plants are still poisonous! Always wear gloves when handling toxic plants, and never allow them to come in contact with food or anything used for food preparation. Have designated labeled tools that are used only for poisonous plants.

✦ Storing

There are three main ways to preserve your herbs after harvesting them: drying, storing in water, and freezing. As a Green Witch, you'll want an extensive apothecary of dried herbs; imagine having rows of labeled jars filled with plant magic! If you're going to keep fresh herbs on hand, you can pop them in water like a bouquet. If you're using herbs for cooking or in potions and brews, freezing may be the best option. To get started, you'll need a variety of containers, some labels, a good chopping knife, and a cutting board.

DRIED

Make sure that your herbs are thoroughly dehydrated before you store them. An excellent way to check is to rub them between your fingers; if they crumble easily, they're dry enough. Dry the leaves whole; they'll last longer and will have a more robust potency and flavor. Store dried plants in airtight containers with tight-fitting lids, like mason jars or ceramic canisters. Avoid using plastic because the chemicals may leach into the herbs. Store dried herbs out of the sunlight and keep them in a cool, dry place. Dried herbs will last 2 to 3 years.

IN WATER

Fresh herbs with soft stems, like mint and dill, can be preserved in water like a flower bouquet and last up to 2 weeks. Wash them with cold water and pat dry, clip the base off the stems, and remove any damaged leaves. Place the stems in a jar with 1 inch of water in the bottom, cover loosely with a plastic bag, and store in the refrigerator. The only exception is basil; it will turn black if refrigerated, so keep your basil bouquet in a glass of water at room temperature. Hard-stemmed herbs like rosemary can be wrapped in a damp paper towel, popped into an airtight container or bag, and stored in the refrigerator.

FREEZING

Freezing is the best method to retain your plant's flavor, scent, and nutrients. Place whole herbs on a baking sheet in a single layer and freeze. Once frozen, put the herbs in labeled containers for freezer storage. Pre-freezing stops herbs from clumping together, making removing a sprig at a time much more manageable. Use straight-walled mason jars and freezer containers, or you could invest in an airtight storage system. Frozen herbs will keep for up to 12 months.

✦ 10 Best Practices for Magical Herbs

Follow these practical ideas for successful herb gardening. Understanding your plants, what they need, and who they are will significantly improve your skill as a Green Witch. Plant and harvest under the influence of the Moon's magic and petition the spirit world for help and guidance. Respect, nourish, and love your plants, and you'll be rewarded with a garden filled with witchy delights!

1. **Know your plants.** Use botanical names for positive identification, and know where, how, and when to plant and harvest.

2. **Empower plants and seeds.** Use visualization to increase potency by concentrating on magical traits during planting and harvesting.

3. **Plant and harvest by the Moon.** Plant aboveground plants on a waxing Moon and belowground crops on a waning Moon; harvest in the moonlight.

4. **Bless your garden regularly.** Attune your soul to your plants with prayers and petitions to the higher powers, ancestors, or nature spirits for your crops to flourish.

5. **Ask permission before you harvest.** Develop your inner listening skills and trust your feelings; how the answer is perceived is different for everyone.

6. **Leave a gift for the Earth when foraging.** Practice reciprocity by leaving an offering for the Earth when wildcrafting.

7. **Be respectful.** Be gentle when cutting or pruning, discard plant material with reverence, handle plants carefully, and inform them of your intentions before doing anything.

8. **Nourish your garden.** Feed the Earth with compost, worm castings, mulch, and organic matter to keep it healthy and productive.

9. **Establish a garden ritual.** Spend time in your garden daily, visiting, observing, and connecting with your plants.

10. **Keep a record.** Create a garden grimoire, or magical manual, to keep track of planting, fertilizing, harvesting times, and garden notes and observations.

CHAPTER THREE

GREEN WITCH SPELLS AND RITUALS

From the beginning, witches have understood and used plants' healing and transforming powers. From the village wise woman concocting healing remedies to the ceremonial magician fuming his magic circle with clouds of sacred smoke, herbs provide a living link to the beliefs and practices of people throughout the ages.

Follow the magic pathway as it winds its way through fifteen spells that will connect you with the ancient knowledge of the plant world. Begin with a simple dedication ritual to mark your commitment; then move on to spells for love, healing, protection, wishes, money, and more.

✦ Plant-Based Magical Practices

The magic of Green Witchcraft harnesses natural plant energy for positive results that cause no harm. Gentle healing and healthy transformation are the goals of Green Witchery as plants manifest through the living Elemental powers of Sunlight, Soil, Water, and Air. Discover plants' subtle nature and unique properties in the tables of correspondence in the Magical Plant Profiles (page 49). Honor the changing seasonal cloak of the Earth Mother as sunlight rises and descends and of the Moon as she waxes and wanes. Transcend the mundane world and explore the realm of spiritual nature.

CLEANSING

Cleansing clears negative energy from your herbs, plants, and spell ingredients. Everything constantly absorbs positive and negative vibes, so it's wise to practice purification before casting a spell. If you don't, your magic may not be as potent; the energies bound to it might work against you. A simple and effective way to cleanse is to place the object with plants that have purifying properties, such as anise, bay leaf, or cedar fronds. Another easy method is to pass it through incense smoke or a candle flame, bury it in earth or salt, or immerse it in water.

SACRED SPACES

Sacred space is an area set aside for and dedicated to spiritual practices and communication with the natural world. You can create sacred space anywhere: in your garden, your home or a forest clearing or on a shelf or windowsill. The easiest way to begin is to make an altar using symbols and objects meaningful to you and your life. If you prefer not to use an altar, you can designate a specific area indoors or out where you find peace and can ground and center yourself.

INTENTION

Intention, in the magical sense, is the conscious creation of the idea or goal of your spell. It's the mind map of what you want to happen and the first step to casting a spell. It is the focal point of the magic at hand. The optimum word is "will": willpower fuels your intention. If you don't believe it, it won't happen—it's as simple as that! It's essential to keep your intention at the forefront of your mind throughout the whole magical process, along with the absolute conviction that you will realize your goal.

THE GREEN WITCH'S HERB AND PLANT ENCYCLOPEDIA

GROUNDING

Grounding is reconnecting and aligning your energy to the Earth. It's easy to do! Outdoors, place your hands flat on the ground, sit with your back to a tree, walk barefoot, lie in the grass or on a sandy beach, or take a walk in a forest. In our modern lives, we have become disconnected from the surface of the Earth and rarely have skin-to-Earth contact. Gardening is the perfect way to achieve grounding, so sink your hands into the soil and receive the positive vibrations that will help alleviate pain, stress, depression, and fatigue. Indoors, use the grounding visualization technique described in chapter 2 (see page 22).

WILD WITCHCRAFT AND THE OUTDOORS

Step outside and enter a sacred world of beauty and magic where wonder, healing, and harmony await. Create a sacred space by planting a Moon Garden filled with lemon balm, white lilies, honesty, and jasmine, or call to the Elements with decorated stones placed in the East, South, West, and North. Make a fairy garden and play with flower spirits and devas. Build an outdoor altar from a recycled tree stump or a wrought iron fire bowl to use as a focal point for your spells and rituals or as a place for offerings and prayers. A gnarled old tree may be adopted in a public park as a symbol of your faith. Whisper your deepest thoughts, tuck prayers in the branches, or honor the tree with gifts and offerings. The sun will guide you into the bright promise of possibility during the daylight. In the moonlight, navigate the spiritual mysteries that can only unfold under the blanket of darkness.

A fallen leaf can be paper for writing prayers, and a fallen twig can transform into a wand or instrument for drawing the Earth's sigils, or magical symbols. Moss and ferns may draw you deeper into the land of the spirit world, and strewn flowers on the ground become a prayer to Gaia as you harvest by the Full Moon's light. Make a wreath of herbs to hang on your door or a circle of flowers to give to a child, pot up some plants for a friend, and save your garden seeds. When it rains, gather the water and keep it for spells or for blessing your plants, and when the wind blows, stand before it to be purified. It's all outdoors, waiting for you to embrace the magic!

VISUALIZING

Visualizing is the conscious creation of a picture in your mind of your spell. The clearer you can "see" it and the more details you can add, the stronger your magic will be. Visualizing activates the subconscious mind and trains the brain to look for and attain resources that support your goal. You may want to imagine your wish as already completed or envision each step you need to take. Either way, mastering the art of visualizing will significantly increase your powers as a witch.

ESSENTIAL EQUIPMENT FOR SPELLCRAFT

Along with practical everyday tools to care for your plants, you'll also need some tools for making magic!

Small bags or pouches. Use drawstring pouches for herb sachets or charm bags, in bath spells, and to carry herbal amulets or talismans.

Fireproof cauldron. Burn dried herbs in the cauldron on a lit charcoal disc. The rising smoke releases your intention into the Universe.

Candles. To boost spells, anoint a candle with oil, roll it in dried herbs that correspond to your intention, or surround it with fresh flowers, leaves, or branches.

Wooden wand. A wand can be foraged from a fallen branch or cut from a living tree and is used to capture and direct energy.

Assorted crystals. Choose a crystal that aligns with your intention or the properties of the plant that you're working with, or use them to heal, honor, and protect your living plants.

TWELVE SPELLS AND RITUALS

Follow these spells and rituals to inspire you with practical ideas for using your herbs and flowers in magic! You may want to begin by devoting yourself to your Green Witch path with the Green Witch Dedication Ritual (page 36), or you may be excited to initiate contact with the beings and spirits that live in and around your garden by trying out the Nature Spirit Meditation (page 38). Go ahead and dive in; you've learned all you need to know in the previous chapters to make beautiful magic. Enchant a fairy altar, protect your home, initiate love and healing, draw wealth, and much more!

GREEN WITCH DEDICATION RITUAL

This simple rite is a lovely way to declare your intention to be a Green Witch. The night of the New Moon represents new beginnings and is the optimal time for this dedication. To set the mood, you may want to bathe in flower- and herb-infused water pre-ritual.

Green candle and holder
Small tray or plate
Fresh-cut flowers and herbs
Lighter
Incense and holder
Vessel of water
Crystal or stone

1. Gather your spell ingredients and find a quiet spot where you won't be disturbed in your garden or home. If you're indoors, surround yourself with as many plants as possible.

2. Spend a few moments grounding your energy (page 33).

3. Place the candle on the tray or plate and surround it with the flowers and herbs. It will be the focal point of your ritual.

4. Light the candle and say:

   By the Element of Fire and the Sun that warms Mother Earth, I am a Green Witch!

5. Carefully pass your hand over the flame. Don't burn yourself.

6. Light the incense and say:

   By the Element of Air and the four strong winds of Mother Earth, I am a Green Witch!

7. Gently waft the incense smoke toward you.

8. Sprinkle some of the water and say:

   By the Element of Water and the lifeblood of Mother Earth, I am a Green Witch!

9. Anoint the back of your hands with the water.

10. Raise the crystal high and say:

    By the Element of Earth and the living body of Mother Earth, I am a Green Witch!

11. With both hands, hold the crystal to your heart.

12. Close your eyes and spend a few moments in meditation. Open your heart and mind for messages from the Green World that you may receive.

GREEN EARTH LOVE SACHET

Create an herbal sachet to draw love or friendship into your life. Remember to never focus on a particular person when casting love spells. Instead, concentrate on the feelings and longings of love or the beautiful traits of your ideal partner. Friday belongs to Venus, the goddess of love, so it's the perfect day for love spells. Rose quartz is also sacred to Venus and will uphold your love intention. Strengthen the magic by timing the spell for when the Moon is waxing (getting bigger). Waxing Moon makes things grow, and this magic's purpose is growing love. Use as many of the dried herbs from the following list as possible. If you don't have them all, that's okay; just use what you have.

6-inch square of green cloth
Rose quartz crystal
12-inch length of green ribbon

DRIED HERBS

* Catnip
* Chamomile
* Cinnamon
* Clove
* Clover
* Geranium
* Jasmine
* Lavender
* Lemon balm
* Rose
* Wild bergamot

1. Gather the ingredients and spend a moment grounding your energy (page 33).

2. Place the crystal in the center of the cloth.

3. Begin adding the dried herbs a pinch at a time while chanting:

   World of green, I call on thee,
   Soon my love shall come to me.
   Herbs of magic, lend your power
   Leaf and root, Earth, and flower.

4. Draw up the four corners of the cloth and tie it closed with the ribbon. Hold the completed sachet to your heart while visualizing the love and happiness it can bring you. Take the sachet outdoors, tuck it in a tree or shrub, or nestle it under a stone, trusting that Mother Earth will carry your spell into the Universe.

NATURE SPIRIT MEDITATION

This meditation will help you connect with the nature spirits living near you. Nature spirits are as old as the land they live upon and are said to be responsible for building and maintaining the plant world—a potent ally for a Green Witch! Foster a relationship with them and be rewarded with their help with your plants, spells, and spiritual alignment. Always address nature spirits with respect and listen to their wisdom as it is whispered to you on the gentle breezes or the songs of wild birds. Make regular offerings to them in a special spot you have chosen to honor them, and soon they'll begin to trust and respect you in return.

Purple candle and holder
Lighter
Chalice of pure water

1. To begin, sit comfortably and ground your energy. Light the candle and use the flame as a focus for your attention. Speak silently or aloud:

   Spirits of Nature, I [name] call to you!
   Guardians of the Earth Mother, Please come; I am here to honor you.

2. Wait for a sign that the nature spirits have arrived. Spiritual communication can be through telepathy, an unusual sound, a touch on your shoulder, or even an animal or bird suddenly appearing. Be open to any signs of their presence and believe that the nature spirits are with you. Silently or aloud, tell them why you want to meet them and ask them who they are. Listen carefully to any messages they wish to give you. Spend time just "being" with them.

3. When you feel that the communication has ended, offer the water. Hold the chalice up to the sky with both hands and say:

   Thank you for your presence,
   Please accept this offering,
   Given with my love and trust.

4. Pour the water onto the Earth and snuff out the candle.

HERBAL WITCH BALL

Make a Witch Ball to protect your home from negative energy. Fillable ornaments can be purchased at craft and dollar stores and look lovely hanging in windows, doorways, and plants. Witch Balls make great gifts, too! When creating your ball, ensure your herbs are very dry, and your crystals are small enough to fit through the ball's opening.

Clear fillable ornament with removable top

Dried bay leaf, for protection

Dried catnip, for happiness

Dried meadowsweet, for happiness

Dried clover flowers, for bringing good luck

Crushed eggshell, for protection

Dried lavender, for peace and harmony

Dried mint, for drawing wealth and riches

Dried rose petals, for love and friendship

Rose quartz crystals, for strengthening relationships

Dried thyme, for good health

Tiny bits of cut-up aluminum foil, for deflecting negative energy

Several 13-inch lengths of green embroidery thread, for trapping bad vibes

Craft glue

12-inch length of ribbon, for hanging

1. Spend a few moments grounding your energy (page 33).

2. Remove the decorative metal cap from the ornament.

3. Crush the herbs in your hands and add them to the Witch Ball one at a time. As you put in each herb, state its purpose aloud to strengthen its magic attributes and tell it what it's supposed to do. Most herbs have several talents, so it helps to let them know what's expected of them!

4. Add the aluminum foil and embroidery thread. Dab a bit of glue on the lid, put it on, and attach the ribbon for hanging. Shake the ball vigorously while chanting 13 times:

   Bay and catnip, clover flowers,
   I call upon your magic powers.
   Shell and rose, crystals, thyme,
   Protect my home and all that's mine.

5. Hang your Witch Ball in a doorway, window, outdoors on a tree branch, or nestle it in a shrub or wreath.

TIP: If you are making this for a friend, change the chant wording to:

   Protect [name's] home and all
   that's theirs.

FOXGLOVE FAIRY ALTAR

Create a magical place for the fairies in your garden. It's not a good idea to invite them into your home; they are mischievous and like to "borrow" things, so it's best if you encourage them to remain outdoors where they belong. Foxglove and thyme are beloved by the fairy folk; when you find it growing wild, it means you're near their home. Keep your fairy altar tidy, or the fairies will be insulted and might stop working with you. Give them offerings of milk, honey, water, flowers, shiny trinkets, and bread; if birds or animals take food offerings, it means that the fairies approve of your gifts. Plant some foxglove and thyme near the altar to show that you care for them. Once you have made steps to encourage the fairy folk, they'll bring enchantment, butterflies, and joy to your garden.

Large stone or stepping stone
Fresh foxglove flowers
Fresh thyme
Tiny dish of milk and honey

1. Find a spot outside that you intuitively "feel" fairy energy and place the stone. Sit comfortably and ground your energy, and then encircle the altar stone with the foxglove flowers and sprinkle it with thyme. Place the dish of milk and honey in the center of the stone.

2. Respectfully ask the fairies to come, tell the fairies that you want to work with them, and ask what they would like from you in return. Explain that you'd like to help them heal the natural world, beginning with your garden. Allow thoughts and images to come with an open mind and heart. When you're ready, thank the fairies for their presence and leave.

3. Make sure to maintain your fairy altar, visit often, and leave offerings.

SALT OF THE EARTH PURIFICATION BATH

Practice self-care by integrating the restorative powers of water, salt, and purifying herbs in a cleansing bath to wash away everything that's bringing you down! If possible, choose a time when the Moon is waning (getting smaller) to align with your intention. Waning Moon energy works best for decreasing, removing, and sending away.

FOR THE EPSOM SALT BLEND

- Glass bowl
- Mixing spoon
- 1 cup Epsom salt
- ¼ cup sea salt
- ¼ cup baking soda
- Mortar and pestle
- Dried star anise
- Dried bay leaf
- Dried peppermint
- Dried lemon peel
- Jar with a tight-fitting lid

FOR THE BATH RITUAL

- White candle and lighter
- Soft music (optional)
- Epsom salt blend
- Lavender essential oil (optional)

4. **To make the Epsom salt blend:** In the glass bowl, combine the Epsom salt, sea salt, and baking soda.

5. Using a mortar and pestle, crush the star anise, bay leaf, peppermint, and lemon peel.

6. Add the mixture to the salts and mix well.

7. Pour the Epsom salt blend into a jar with a lid and seal.

8. **To perform the bath ritual:** Light the candle, place it in a safe place, dim the lights, and turn on the music (if using).

9. Spend a few moments grounding your energy (page 33).

10. Start running the water and add the Epsom salt blend with a few drops of the essential oil (if using).

11. Get into the tub and imagine the scented bathwater dissolving and neutralizing all the unwanted baneful energy you have accumulated over time. Try to dedicate 20 minutes or so to the ritual to maximize its benefits.

12. When you're ready, pull the plug and visualize the unwanted energy flowing down the drain to be absorbed and neutralized by the Earth.

LEMON BALM HEALING POPPET

Poppet dolls are simple to make and very effective for healing magic. If you or a friend are under the weather, whip up a little poppet friend to help you feel better! Cast this spell on a Monday, a day associated with healing and family.

Felt pen

Green fabric

Scissors

Needle and thread

Paper and pen

Cotton or other stuffing material

4 tablespoons dried lemon balm

1. Spend a few moments grounding your energy (page 33).

2. Draw and cut two poppet shapes out of the fabric. Make each poppet shape as a very rounded human with chunky arms and legs; skinny arms and legs are hard to stuff.

3. Stitch the poppet together, leaving an opening at the top of the head.

4. On a small piece of parchment, write the name of the person you want to heal.

5. Begin stuffing the poppet with the cotton, adding a pinch of lemon balm with each handful of stuffing. While working, visualize the poppet filling with healing energy.

6. Once you reach the center of the chest (where the heart is), insert the parchment, and then continue stuffing until the poppet is full.

7. Sew the opening shut; then hold the poppet to your heart and say:

> *Little poppet, healing friend,*
> *[name of the person to be healed]*
> *is on the mend.*
> *Lemon balm buried deep inside,*
> *Healing energy now abides.*

8. Find a special place to keep the poppet while it does its magic. Place it on your altar or among your plants, or you may want to create its own sacred space by placing it on a cloth and surrounding it with crystals, stones, plants, herbs, or anything else that resonates with your healing intention.

PERIWINKLE LILAC SALT

Create this enchanting potion under the Full Moon's light when psychic power is at its peak to enhance your clairvoyant abilities, grow your spiritual wisdom, power up divination, and enhance your focus during meditation. This fascinating potion combines salt with the intuitive vibrations of the purple color found in periwinkle, lilac, and amethyst crystals. If you don't have periwinkle growing, take a walk in your neighborhood, look in shady areas for its distinctive purple flowers, and pick a few flowers.

Mortar and pestle

1 tablespoon dried periwinkle

1 tablespoon dried lilac

2 tablespoons sea salt

1 drop purple food coloring

Wooden spoon

Glass bottle or jar with lid

Amethyst crystal

1. Spend a few moments grounding your energy (page 33).

2. Using a mortar and pestle, grind the periwinkle and lilac flowers to a fine powder. While grinding, move your pestle clockwise to keep your intention positive and your focus on the potion's spiritual goal.

3. Once the herbs are finely ground, add the sea salt and food coloring, stirring gently with the wooden spoon.

4. Pour the salt mixture into the jar, add the amethyst crystal, and then seal and label the bottle.

5. To use the periwinkle lilac salt:

   - *Sprinkle a tiny bit on divination tools before use.*
   - *Place under your pillow to induce psychic dreams.*
   - *Add to water to bless and charge it before spellcasting.*
   - *Add to dream sachets, magic bags, and pouches.*
   - *Dampen a purple candle with oil and roll it in the salt to enhance intuitive magic.*
   - *Place with purple crystals or flowers to cleanse and charge them.*
   - *Sprinkle on your hands before handling tarot cards.*
   - *Mix with incense burned for spiritual intentions.*
   - *Pour onto a plate or tray and draw runes or symbols for spells and rituals.*
   - *Hold a pinch in your hand to help center and ground your energy.*
   - *Sprinkle it in a circle around you before meditation.*

HONEYSUCKLE MONEY MAGNET

Want a permanent honeysuckle money magnet in your home or garden to draw wealth and riches your way? Use a living honeysuckle plant, either potted or in-ground, to make the magic come alive. Do this spell on a Thursday, the best day of the week to manifest money! Six is the magic number of prosperity.

Paper and pen
Live honeysuckle plant
6 malachite crystals or any green crystals
Green candle and holder
Candle carving tool
Olive oil
Dried peppermint
Lighter
6 coins
6 green ribbons cut into 12-inch lengths

1. Spend a few moments grounding your energy (page 33).

2. Write your money wishes on the paper, fold it in half, and place it beside the honeysuckle plant. Place the crystals on top of the paper.

3. Carve your name, the date, and a dollar sign or money symbol on the candle.

4. Rub the candle with olive oil, roll it in dried peppermint, place it in the holder, and light it. Chant six times:

   Candle flame burning bright,
   Let money appear within my sight.

5. Place the coins around the bottom of the plant and chant six times:

   Nickels, dimes, and pennies, too,
   What I want will come true!

6. Sprinkle dried peppermint in a circle around the honeysuckle and chant six times:

   Mint will help the money grow,
   It comes to me in a steady flow.

7. Draw a symbol or write a money request on the ribbons and tie them to the honeysuckle branches. Chant six times:

   Element of Air, I ask of thee,
   Blow my wishes home to me!

8. Allow the candle to burn down completely.

9. Reinforce your spell by regularly giving your honeysuckle offerings of mint, cinnamon sticks, or dried nutmeg. Refresh the ribbons occasionally and continue to add coins and green stones to keep the magic alive!

PLANT YOUR WISHES SEED SPELL

Make your dreams come true with this classic Green Witch wishing spell. When the energies of growth are the strongest during the New Moon, you'll plant a seed enchanted with your desire and then watch the magic grow. Be sure to choose plant seeds that align with your wishes, like heliotrope for dreams or goldenrod for money. Check out the Magical Plant Profile section of this book (see page 49) for more ideas.

Parchment paper and pen

Plant pot

Black felt pen

Potting soil

Package of seeds or a bulb

Full watering can

1. Spend a few moments grounding your energy (page 33).

2. Inscribe your wishes on a small piece of parchment paper and place it at the bottom of the plant pot.

3. With the felt pen, write on the inside of the pot. Put your name and the date along with any prayers, chants, or symbols that express your wish.

4. Fill the pot with potting soil, and follow the seed package's instructions as you plant your seed. It's a good idea to plant three seeds just in case one or two don't germinate. If all three plants begin to grow, you can keep the most vigorous plant and pinch out the weaker ones.

5. As you firm the soil over the seeds, chant three times:

   Mother Earth, hear my prayer.
   I place this seed into your care.
   Help it to grow up strong and true.
   This is what I ask of you!

6. Bless the water in the watering can by placing your hands over it. Visualize Earth energy flowing up from the ground and into your hands. As you direct the power into the water, say:

   Mother Earth, bless this water so that it may bring these seeds to life.

7. Moisten the soil well, and then set the pot in a sunny, warm place.

8. Carefully nurture and tend your plant, for your wish will come true as the plant grows and flourishes!

HAPPY HERBS SPELL JAR

Make your house a happy place using herbs and crystals to create a spell jar that will draw in good vibes.

Jar with lid

Smiley face drawing on paper

Dried lavender

Dried lemon peel

Dried basil

Dried thyme

Dried catnip

Dried mugwort

Dried marjoram

Dried meadowsweet

Blue lace agate crystals

Rose quartz crystals

1 teaspoon honey

Drop of water that has been in sunlight for 6 hours

Pink candle and lighter

Ribbon with charms

1. Spend a few moments grounding your energy (page 33).

2. Put the smiley face paper in the bottom of the jar and begin adding the ingredients in the listed order.

3. As you add ingredients to the spell jar, keep your focus on happiness!

4. Chant this rhyme as you fill the jar:

   Lavender, the happy herb, with lemon peel, draws friends and love.

   Basil for a lucky home, and thyme brings charms to everyone!

   Catnip joy and comfort bring, while sister mugwort adds protection.

   Marjoram, the herb of health, lives with peaceful meadowsweet.

   Agate crystals free the soul, and rose quartz calms and soothes.

   Honey sweetens all, and a drop of the sun for strength and light.

5. Put the lid on the jar.

6. Light the candle, hold it over the lid, and let the wax drip and flow to seal the jar lid.

7. String charms (triquetra, pentacle, beads, stones, etc.) on the ribbon, and then tie it to the top of the jar.

8. Hold the jar in both hands for a few moments and visualize your home filled with joy and harmony!

9. Place your Happy Herbs Spell Jar in a prominent place where you'll see it daily and be reminded to uphold the spell by keeping your space positive and joyful.

MOONBEAMS AND MUGWORT DREAM PILLOW

Make this herbal dream pillow to encourage restful sleep and sweet dreams. Sewing is a form of knot magic, and each stitch gives you a chance to strengthen the spell, as the meditative qualities of stitching free you to insert your intention with every stab of the needle. A dream pillow may be the perfect solution if you have a child who has sleepless nights or nightmares. Dream pillows are easy to make and an excellent way to share your garden's bounty with friends and family. If you're making one as a gift, tie a pretty ribbon around it and attach a hangtag with ingredients and instructions. The best time for this garden craft is under the dreamy influence of the Full Moon.

Pretty fabric cut into 2 (6-inch) squares

Needle and thread

Knitting needle or chopstick

1 cup dried mugwort

½ cup dried rose petals

⅓ cup dried sage

⅓ cup dried lavender

⅓ cup dried catnip

1 tablespoon dried mint

Ribbon (optional)

Hangtag (optional)

1. Spend a few moments grounding your energy (page 33).

2. Place the squares of fabric with right sides together and sew around the edges using a ½-inch seam allowance. Leave a 2-inch opening for adding the herbs. With each stitch, focus on dreaming, healing, and soothing.

3. Turn the pillow right-side out and push the corners out completely with a chopstick or knitting needle so they're nice and neat.

4. Fill the pillow with the herbs, and then sew it closed.

5. To use the dream pillow, gently squeeze it to activate the herbs, and then place it inside your pillowcase before sleep.

PART II

MAGICAL PLANT PROFILES

CAUTION: Always ensure accurate identification of a plant before handling, whether you are foraging it or growing it yourself. Use a field guide (see Resources, page 207) for positive identification and know the scientific name. Take precautions when handling and using any plants with which you are unfamiliar.

ACONITE

Aconitum napellus

Size: 2 to 5 feet

Parts Used: Leaves, flowers

Safety Considerations: Poisonous to humans and pets. Avoid touching aconite with bare skin; always wear gloves when handling.

Planetary Ruler: Saturn

Moon Phase: Waning

Element: Water

Zodiac Sign: Scorpio

Gender: Feminine

Deity: Hecate, Thor

Lore: Aconite was used to poison arrows and spears for hunting and battle. Athena sprinkled the goddess Arachne with aconite juice and turned her into a spider. Aconite is one of the ingredients mentioned in Witch's Flying Oil.

Magical Purpose: Consecration, invisibility, protection

MAGICAL AMPLIFIERS

- ♦ **Angel:** Azrael
- ♦ **Chakra:** Root
- ♦ **Crystals:** Hematite, jet, obsidian
- ♦ **Tarot:** Death
- ♦ **Sacred to:** Samhain

FOR GARDENING

Aconite, or monkshood, is a tall perennial with blue, hood-shaped flowers blooming in late summer.

Suggested Varieties for Beginners: Blue Sceptre, Newry Blue

Location: USDA Plant Hardiness Zone 3–7

Light: Full sun to part shade

Water and Food: Generous watering, add compost and fertilizer in the spring

Soil, Pot, Cultivation: Moist, well-drained loamy soil; grow in 14-inch pots; cut back to ground level after the first frost

AFRICAN VIOLET

Saintpaulia ionantha

Size: 6 to 8 inches

Parts Used: Flowers

Safety Considerations: Edible. Nontoxic for humans and pets.

Planetary Ruler: Venus

Moon Phase: Full

Element: Water

Zodiac Sign: Cancer

Gender: Feminine

Deity: Aphrodite, Venus

Lore: African violets are associated with motherhood and are a popular gift to mothers worldwide.

Magical Purpose: Spirituality, protection

MAGICAL AMPLIFIERS

- ♦ **Angel:** Gabriel
- ♦ **Chakra:** Solar Plexus
- ♦ **Crystals:** Labradorite, carnelian, citrine
- ♦ **Tarot:** Strength

DIY TIP: Put dried African violet flowers in an organza bag and place the bag under your pillow to ward off nightmares or carry it with you to protect against negative energy.

FOR GARDENING

African violets are among the most popular houseplants, with flowers that bloom several times a year.

Suggested Varieties for Beginners: Cherry Princess, Summer Twilight

Location: Indoor houseplant

Light: Bright, indirect light

Water and Food: Keep moist but well drained; feed with African violet fertilizer every 2 weeks

Soil, Pot, Cultivation: Well-drained potting soil; allow the plant to become root-bound before repotting; baby plants sometimes grow from side shoots and can be removed and potted

AGRIMONY

Agrimonia gryposepala

Size: 30 inches

Parts Used: Whole herb

Safety Considerations: Edible. For humans, nontoxic in small amounts; for pets, toxic.

Planetary Ruler: Jupiter, Mercury

Moon Phase: Waning

Element: Air

Zodiac Sign: Cancer

Gender: Masculine

Deity: Mithras

Lore: One of agrimony's earliest common names was "fairy's wand," believed to cure people suffering from unexplained sickness. An infusion made from the leaves and seeds called "musket-shot water" was used to heal wounds.

Magical Purpose: Hex-breaking, protection, sleep

MAGICAL AMPLIFIERS

- ♦ **Angel:** Michael
- ♦ **Chakra:** Throat
- ♦ **Crystal:** Jet
- ♦ **Tarot:** Temperance

FOR FORAGING

A tea can be made of leaves and flowers to ease an upset stomach. Forage throughout North America. USDA Plant Hardiness Zone 6–9

DIY TIP: Make a tincture of agrimony for fevers, colds, and sore throats. Agrimony tea is a heart tonic, sedative, and antihistamine.

ALOE

Aloe vera

Size: 1 to 2 feet

Parts Used: Leaves, root

Safety Considerations: Edible. For humans, nontoxic externally or if ingested in small amounts; for pets, mild to moderately toxic.

Planetary Ruler: Moon, Venus

Moon Phase: Full

Element: Water

Zodiac Sign: Scorpio, Pisces, Cancer

Gender: Feminine

Deity: Diana, Venus

Lore: Alexander the Great went to war to secure supplies of aloe to treat his wounded soldiers.

Magical Purpose: Friendship, healing, love, protection, purification, sorrow

MAGICAL AMPLIFIERS

♦ **Angel:** Gabriel
♦ **Chakras:** Third Eye, Heart
♦ **Crystals:** Clear quartz, onyx
♦ **Tarot:** The Sun

DIY TIP: Apply the gel from a cut leaf to treat skin irritation.

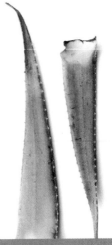

FOR GARDENING

Aloe is an upright succulent plant with pale green fleshy leaves; it's easy to grow as a houseplant.

Location: USDA Plant Hardiness Zone 8–11; grow as a houseplant in cooler zones

Light: 4 hours minimum

Water and Food: Light watering, let the soil dry out between waterings; use liquid fertilizer monthly

Soil, Pot, Cultivation: Succulent potting mix, grow in terra-cotta pot, replant the pups growing at the base of the plant

AMERICAN ELM

Ulmus americana

Size: 60 to 80 feet

Parts Used: Leaves, bark

Safety Considerations: Edible. Nontoxic for humans and pets.

Planetary Ruler: Saturn

Moon Phase: Full

Elements: Air, Earth, Water

Zodiac Sign: Capricorn, Sagittarius

Gender: Feminine

Deity: Cerridwen, Danu, Loki

Lore: The Celts associated elm with elves and the passage to the Underworld. Artemis practiced using her silver bow and arrows by shooting at an elm tree.

Magical Purpose: Love, wisdom

MAGICAL AMPLIFIERS

♦ **Angel:** Chamuel
♦ **Chakra:** Heart
♦ **Crystals:** Rose quartz, rhodonite, pink kunzite
♦ **Tarot:** Wheel of Fortune

FOR FORAGING

The bark of an elm is rough and coarse, and the oval leaves have jagged edges and are pointed at the end. Forage in the eastern and central United States. USDA Plant Hardiness Zone 2-9

DIY TIP: Ask the elm permission to take a small branch as a magic wand to enhance stability, grounding, and focus in your spells and rituals.

ANGELICA

Angelica archangelica

Size: 3 to 6 feet

Parts Used: Root, stems, leaves, seeds

Safety Considerations: Edible. Nontoxic for humans and pets. May cause skin sensitivity; wear gloves when handling.

Planetary Ruler: Sun

Moon Phase: Waning

Element: Fire

Zodiac Sign: Aries, Leo

Gender: Masculine

Deity: Angels

Lore: Angelica may have originated in the lost city of Atlantis. It's been called the "most powerful" herb and "Root of the Holy Ghost."

Magical Purpose: Exorcism, protection, luck, healing, visions

MAGICAL AMPLIFIERS

- **Angel:** Michael
- **Chakra:** Third Eye
- **Crystals:** Cat's-eye, jasper
- **Tarot:** The Sun
- **Sacred to:** Beltane, Imbolc, Samhain

> **DIY TIP:** Harvest leaves and flowers anytime, dig roots in early spring, and cut stalks in late spring.

FOR GARDENING

Angelica is easy to grow, but don't let it dry out. It can be grown from seed and readily reseeds itself.

Suggested Varieties for Beginners: Common angelica

Location: USDA Plant Hardiness Zone 4-9

Light: Part shade to full sun

Water and Food: Regular watering, add compost in spring and balanced fertilizer monthly

Soil, Pot, Cultivation: Well-drained, rich soil; grow in 16-inch pots; self-seeds in the garden

ASH

Fraxinus excelsior

Size: 32 to 100 feet

Parts Used: Leaves, bark

Safety Considerations: Edible. Nontoxic for humans and pets.

Planetary Ruler: Sun

Moon Phase: Waxing

Element: Fire

Zodiac Sign: Sagittarius

Gender: Masculine

Deity: Uranus, Thor, Mars, Neptune

Lore: Ash is the symbolic female counterpart to the masculine oak. In Norse mythology, Odin hung upon an ash tree for three days and nights until the twigs formed into the runic alphabet.

Magical Purpose: Protection, prosperity, health

MAGICAL AMPLIFIERS

- **Angel:** Raphael
- **Chakra:** Heart
- **Crystals:** Amethyst, moonstone, obsidian
- **Tarot:** The Star

FOR FORAGING

The long petal-shaped fruit can be harvested and safely eaten in spring. Forage throughout North America. USDA Plant Hardiness Zone 2–5

DIY TIP: To make a charm, cut an ash branch (with permission) and carve protective symbols like pentagrams, spirals, or triquetras on the twig. Wrap it with a blue ribbon and hang the charm over your front door.

ASTER

Symphyotrichum spp.

Size: 1 to 6 feet

Parts Used: Flowers, leaves, root

Safety Considerations: Nontoxic for humans and pets.

Planetary Ruler: Venus

Moon Phase: Waxing

Element: Water

Zodiac Sign: Sagittarius, Virgo

Gender: Feminine

Deity: Venus, Astraea

Lore: Asters got their name from the Greek goddess Astraea, which means "star." Astraea was sad because there weren't many stars in the night sky and began to cry; when her tears fell to Earth, they transformed into beautiful aster flowers.

Magical Purpose: Love, peace, happiness, truth

MAGICAL AMPLIFIERS

♦ **Angel:** Gabriel
♦ **Chakra:** Heart
♦ **Crystals:** Blue lace agate, selenite
♦ **Tarot:** The Empress
♦ **Sacred to:** Fairies

DIY TIP: Dry flower stems upside down in a bundle for dried flower arrangements.

FOR GARDENING

Asters like to be cool and moist; mulch plants and protect from the midday sun.

Suggested Varieties for Beginners: New England aster

Location: USDA Plant Hardiness Zone 3–8

Light: Full sun to part sun

Water and Food: Generous watering, add compost or balanced fertilizer in spring

Soil, Pot, Cultivation: Well-drained soil, grow in 18-inch pots, divide every 2 years

BASIL

Ocimum basilicum

Size: 1 to 2 feet

Parts Used: Leaves

Safety Considerations: Edible. Nontoxic for humans and pets.

Planetary Ruler: Mars

Moon Phase: Waxing

Element: Fire

Zodiac Sign: Aries, Scorpio

Gender: Masculine

Deity: Lakshmi

Lore: Basil has a conflicted history; European folklore claims that it is beloved by the devil and must be planted while cursing, yet basil was also believed to cause people to fall madly in love!

Magical Purpose: Money, luck, quarrels

MAGICAL AMPLIFIERS

◆ **Angel:** Chamuel
◆ **Chakra:** Root
◆ **Crystals:** Aventurine, bloodstone, emerald
◆ **Tarot:** The Emperor
◆ **Sacred to:** Imbolc

DIY TIP: Carry dried basil in your wallet to attract money or sprinkle it around your home for protection. Burn as an exorcism incense.

FOR GARDENING

Basil is a tender annual that likes to be kept warm and moist.

Suggested Varieties for Beginners: Sweet basil, lemon basil

Location: USDA Plant Hardiness Zone 10–11; grow as an annual in cooler zones

Light: Full sun

Water and Food: Generous watering, compost in spring, fertilize sparingly

Soil, Pot, Cultivation: Moist, rich, well-drained soil; grow in pots 8 inches deep; mulch to retain moisture

THE GREEN WITCH'S HERB AND PLANT ENCYCLOPEDIA

BAY

Laurus nobilis

Size: 10 to 25 feet

Parts Used: Leaves, stems, branches

Safety Considerations: Edible. Toxic to pets, nontoxic for humans.

Planetary Ruler: Sun

Moon Phase: Waxing

Element: Fire

Zodiac Sign: Capricorn

Gender: Masculine

Deity: Daphne, Apollo

Lore: The Oracles of Delphi chewed bay leaves to put them into a trance before uttering riddles and prophecies. Apollo is often depicted wearing a bay leaf crown.

Magical Purpose: Protection, prophecy, healing, purification, divination

MAGICAL AMPLIFIERS

- **Angels:** Ariel, Gabriel
- **Chakra:** Solar Plexus
- **Crystals:** Amethyst, fluorite, hematite
- **Tarot:** The Sun

> **DIY TIP:** Write spells and prayers on the leaves. Keep a dried bay leaf with your tarot cards and other divination tools to heighten clairvoyance.

FOR GARDENING

Bay is fast-growing and needs winter protection. For colder climates, grow in pots.

Suggested Varieties for Beginners: *Laurus nobilis*

Location: USDA Plant Hardiness Zone 8–10

Light: Full sun

Water and Food: Regular watering, avoid soggy roots, add compost and balanced fertilizer in spring, and feed potted laurel once a month

Soil, Pot, Cultivation: Organic compost and sand mixture, grow in 24-inch pot, prune to keep the shape

BEAN

Phaseolus spp.

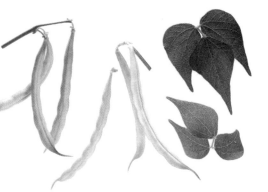

Size: 4 feet

Parts Used: Pods, beans

Safety Considerations: Edible. Nontoxic for humans and pets.

Planetary Ruler: Mercury

Moon Phase: Waxing

Element: Air

Zodiac Sign: Libra

Gender: Masculine

Deity: Demeter

Lore: Ancient Egyptians believed that bean pods contained the souls of the dead, and it was forbidden to eat them or destroy bean plants.

Magical Purpose: Wisdom, divination, prosperity

MAGICAL AMPLIFIERS

♦ **Angel:** Raphael
♦ **Chakra:** Third Eye
♦ **Crystals:** Aquamarine, smoky quartz, sodalite
♦ **Tarot:** The Magician
♦ **Sacred to:** Samhain

DIY TIP: At the end of the season, pick and dry overgrown pods, and remove and store the dried beans.

FOR GARDENING

Bean requires warm soil to germinate; sow seeds directly into the garden. Pole beans need a structure to support them.

Suggested Varieties for Beginners: Blue Lake, Provider, Kentucky Wonder

Location: USDA Plant Hardiness Zone 2–11

Light: Full sun

Water and Food: Deeply water, avoid manure or nitrogen fertilizer, and fertilize monthly

Soil, Pot, Cultivation: Average soil, grow bush beans in 8-inch pots and pole beans in 14-inch pots, keep the soil moist, harvest regularly

BEE BALM

Monarda fistulosa

Size: 4 feet

Parts Used: Flowers, leaves

Safety Considerations: Edible. Nontoxic for humans and pets.

Planetary Ruler: Mercury

Moon Phase: New

Element: Air

Zodiac Sign: Gemini

Gender: Masculine

Deity: Demeter, Artemis

Lore: Also called wild bergamot and horsemint, bee balm was a tea replacement for English tea after the Boston Tea Party.

Magical Purpose: Purification, relaxation, intellect, success

MAGICAL AMPLIFIERS

- ◆ **Angel:** Raphael
- ◆ **Chakra:** Throat
- ◆ **Crystals:** Moss agate, rose quartz
- ◆ **Tarot:** The Sun

DIY TIP: Use fresh leaves on wounds as an antiseptic. Carry dried bee balm in a sachet for success.

FOR GARDENING

Bee balm is a member of the mint family with clusters of pink, red, or purple flowers and strongly scented leaves. It will spread quickly underground through slender rhizomes.

Suggested Varieties for Beginners: Marshall's Delight, Jacob Cline

Location: USDA Plant Hardiness Zone 3–9

Light: Light shade in hot climates

Water and Food: Regular watering, add compost in spring and balanced fertilizer monthly

Soil, Pot, Cultivation: Rich, moist soil, does not tolerate dry conditions; grow in 15-inch pot; divide roots every 3 to 4 years

BELLADONNA

Atropa belladonna

Size: 3 to 4 feet

Parts Used: Flowers, leaves, fruit, root

Safety Considerations: Poisonous to humans and pets. All parts are deadly poison if ingested; always wear gloves and long sleeves when handling.

Planetary Ruler: Saturn

Moon Phase: Waning

Element: Water

Zodiac Sign: Scorpio

Gender: Feminine

Deity: Bellona, Circe, Hecate

Lore: During the Middle Ages, a beauty potion was made of belladonna leaves and berries to redden ladies' cheeks. The more sinister use was as a poison of choice for assassins and criminals. Witchcraft lore states that belladonna must be sung to as it's harvested; it's also believed to be one of the ingredients in Witch's Flying Oil.

Magical Purpose: Astral travel, consecration, divination, visions

MAGICAL AMPLIFIERS

- ◆ **Angel:** Gabriel
- ◆ **Chakra:** Crown
- ◆ **Crystals:** Onyx
- ◆ **Tarot:** The Fool

FOR FORAGING

Belladonna is a perennial woody shrub with bell-shaped dull purple flowers and shiny black berries. USDA Plant Hardiness Zone 6-9

DIY TIP: Consecrate and charge tools dedicated to spirit work with incense made of dried belladonna leaves. Belladonna should only be burned outdoors; the smoke is highly toxic.

BINDWEED

Calystegia sepium

Size: 9 feet

Parts Used: Flowers, seeds

Safety Considerations: For humans, seeds are toxic but leaves are nontoxic; for pets, toxic.

Planetary Ruler: Saturn

Moon Phase: Full

Element: Water

Zodiac Sign: Scorpio

Gender: Feminine

Deity: Nyx

Lore: Morning glory is beloved by the fairy folk, and for centuries, it has been planted in gardens to attract them.

Magical Purpose: Binding spells, bridge to other realms

MAGICAL AMPLIFIERS

- ◆ **Angel:** Gabriel
- ◆ **Chakra:** Crown
- ◆ **Crystals:** Herkimer diamond, lodestone, onyx
- ◆ **Tarot:** The World

FOR GARDENING

Bindweed is invasive, so be careful where you plant it. Forage throughout North America along streams, thickets, roadsides, and waste areas. USDA Plant Hardiness Zone 4-8.

DIY TIP: Bindweed is a substitution for High John the Conqueror root. Ropes made from the vines are very powerful when used for binding and protection spells.

BLACK COHOSH
Cimicifuga racemosa

Size: 4 to 6 feet

Parts Used: Root

Safety Considerations: Edible. Non-toxic in small amounts for both humans and pets.

Planetary Ruler: Pluto

Moon Phase: Waxing, Waning

Element: Fire

Zodiac Sign: Scorpio

Gender: Masculine

Deity: Mother Goddess

Lore: Black cohosh was an essential plant for the Indigenous people living in the Ohio Valley and used to help alleviate menstruation pain and rheumatism; it often grew near their settlements.

Magical Purpose: Love, courage, protection, potency, banishing

MAGICAL AMPLIFIERS

- **Angel:** Azrael
- **Chakra:** Root
- **Crystals:** Bloodstone, garnet, labradorite
- **Tarot:** Strength

DIY TIP: Make a cleansing, purifying room spray by adding the dried root to a spray bottle filled with equal parts of distilled water and witch hazel.

FOR GARDENING

Protect from direct sun and keep the soil moist; it may require staking.

Suggested Varieties for Beginners: Brunette, Black Beauty

Location: USDA Plant Hardiness Zone 4–8

Light: Shade to part shade

Water and Food: Regular watering, add compost in spring

Soil, Pot, Cultivation: Rich, moist soil, high in organic matter; large roots don't do well in containers; divide rhizomes in spring or fall

BLACKBERRY

Rubus

Size: 3 to 4 feet

Parts Used: Leaves, fruit

Safety Considerations: Edible. Nontoxic for humans and pets.

Planetary Ruler: Venus

Moon Phase: Full

Element: Water

Zodiac Sign: Aries, Scorpio, Taurus

Gender: Feminine

Deity: Brigid, Dionysus, Freya, Osiris

Lore: English folklore states that passing under a blackberry branch will cure illness. The Celts believed that the berries were fairy food, and it was unlucky to eat them.

Magical Purpose: Communication, death, healing, prosperity, spirits

MAGICAL AMPLIFIERS

- ♦ **Angel:** Azrael
- ♦ **Chakra:** Throat
- ♦ **Crystals:** Bloodstone, emerald, jade, sapphire, zircon
- ♦ **Tarot:** Death
- ♦ **Sacred to:** Lughnasadh, Mabon

DIY TIP: Use a blackberry thorn as a tool to inscribe candles. Blackberry leaf tea is thought to be an aphrodisiac.

FOR GARDENING

Blackberries are easy to grow; plant when canes are dormant. To prevent the spread of disease, don't plant near wild blackberries.

Suggested Varieties for Beginners: Triple Crown

Location: USDA Plant Hardiness Zone 4–10

Light: Full sun

Water and Food: Regular watering, fertilize when flowers appear

Soil, Pot, Cultivation: Well-drained soil with organic matter and mulch, grow in a 5-gallon pot, prune according to variety

BLADDERWRACK

Fucus vesiculosus

Size: 3 feet

Parts Used: Whole plant

Safety Considerations: Edible. Nontoxic for humans and pets.

Planetary Ruler: Moon

Moon Phase: Waxing

Element: Water

Zodiac Sign: Cancer

Gender: Feminine

Deity: Luna

Lore: It was believed that throwing seaweed into the waves summoned a mermaid who would help you with your magic. Greek magicians twirled strands of seaweed over their heads while whistling to conjure a storm.

Magical Purpose: Protection, sea magic, wind spells

MAGICAL AMPLIFIERS

♦ **Angel:** Uriel
♦ **Chakra:** Sacral
♦ **Crystals:** Abalone, coral, pearl
♦ **Tarot:** Strength

FOR FORAGING

Gather during low tide. You will need a bucket and knife. Rinse bladderwrack well before cooking. Dry on racks or cookie sheets for magical applications. Found along the coastlines of the Atlantic and Pacific Oceans.

DIY TIP: Hang a braid of seaweed at your front door to ward off negative energy. Add dried seaweed to protection sachets and keep a jar on your kitchen windowsill to bring in good luck.

BLEEDING HEART

Lamprocapnos spectabilis

Size: 6 to 36 inches

Parts Used: Flowers

Safety Considerations: Toxic for humans and pets. All parts of the plant are toxic when ingested, and touching the plant may cause skin irritation. Always wear gloves when handling.

Planetary Ruler: Venus

Moon Phase: Waxing

Element: Water

Zodiac Sign: Cancer

Gender: Feminine

Deity: Aphrodite

Lore: Take off the two outer flower petals, set them on their sides, and reveal two pink rabbits; pull off the two white inner petals and show a pair of earrings; the remaining center of the flower is a heart.

Magical Purpose: Love, divination

MAGICAL AMPLIFIERS

- ◆ **Angel:** Chamuel
- ◆ **Chakra:** Heart
- ◆ **Crystals:** Emerald, rose quartz, clear quartz
- ◆ **Tarot:** The Lovers

DIY TIP: For love divination, crush a bleeding heart flower: if the juice is red, you are loved; if the liquid is white, you are not loved.

FOR GARDENING

Bleeding hearts are shade-loving plants that bloom for several weeks in the spring. The delicate flowers require protection from strong winds and hot sun.

Suggested Varieties for Beginners: Valentine, Gold Heart

Location: USDA Plant Hardiness Zone 2–9

Light: Part shade

Water and Food: Generous watering, add compost in the spring

Soil, Pot, Cultivation: Moist, humus-rich soil; grow in 12-inch pots; cut the stems back in the fall

BLESSED THISTLE

Cnicus benedictus

Size: 2 feet

Parts Used: Leaves, thistles

Safety Considerations: Nontoxic for humans and pets.

Planetary Ruler: Mars

Moon Phase: Waxing

Element: Fire

Zodiac Sign: Leo

Gender: Masculine

Deity: Minerva, Thor

Lore: In the language of flowers, the thistle is a flower of intrusion and warning. Throwing thistle into a fire will prevent lightning from striking.

Magical Purpose: Purification, hex-breaking

MAGICAL AMPLIFIERS

- **Angel:** Michael
- **Chakra:** Throat
- **Crystals:** Alexandrite, fire opal, fluorite
- **Tarot:** The Devil
- **Sacred to:** Mabon

FOR FORAGING

Blessed thistle is a very easy-to-grow annual with huge, interesting-looking flowers surrounded by a "crown of thorns." Harvest flowers to prevent the plant from spreading; it can be invasive. Forage throughout North America. USDA Plant Hardiness Zone 5–9

DIY TIP: Create an anti-hexing poppet by stuffing it with dried thistle flowers.

BLUEBERRY

Vaccinium

Size: 2 to 12 feet

Parts Used: Berries

Safety Considerations: Edible. Nontoxic for humans and pets.

Planetary Ruler: Moon, Venus

Moon Phase: Full

Elements: Water, Earth

Zodiac Sign: Cancer, Pisces

Gender: Feminine

Deity: Selene, Luna, Herne

Lore: Blueberries may have been the first edible fruits discovered after the last ice age.

Magical Purpose: Protection

FOR GARDENING

Plant blueberries in the spring; they are slow growing and may take a few years before producing berries.

Suggested Varieties for Beginners: Biloxi, Bluecrop, Blueray

Location: USDA Plant Hardiness Zone 3–10, depending on the variety

Light: Full sun

Water and Food: Regular watering, use acidic plant fertilizer

Soil, Pot, Cultivation: Well-drained, acidic soil; grow in 18-inch pots; add mulch to protect shallow roots

MAGICAL AMPLIFIERS

♦ **Angel:** Gabriel

♦ **Chakra:** Heart

♦ **Crystals:** Clear quartz, Herkimer diamond, onyx

♦ **Tarot:** The Moon

DIY TIP: Dry blueberries, crush them in a mortar and pestle, and mix with sea salt. Sprinkle the mixture anywhere you need protection.

BORAGE

Borago officinalis

Size: 1 to 3 feet

Parts Used: Young leaves, flowers

Safety Considerations: Edible. Toxic to pets, nontoxic for humans.

Planetary Ruler: Jupiter

Moon Phase: New

Element: Air

Zodiac Sign: Leo, Aquarius

Gender: Masculine

Deity: Euphrosyne

Lore: The word *borage* may have come from the Celtic *borrach*, meaning "courage." The Druids consecrated their weapons with the flower petals and drank borage-infused wine to gain courage before going into battle.

Magical Purpose: Courage, psychic powers, happiness, peace

MAGICAL AMPLIFIERS

♦ **Angel:** Michael
♦ **Chakra:** Solar Plexus
♦ **Crystals:** Carnelian, hematite, sardonyx
♦ **Tarot:** The Star
♦ **Sacred to:** Summer Solstice

FOR GARDENING

Borage grows quickly and has clusters of blue flowers that bees love.

Suggested Varieties for Beginners: Common borage

Location: USDA Plant Hardiness Zone 2–11

Light: Full sun to part shade

Water and Food: Regular watering, drought tolerant, fertilize sparingly

Soil, Pot, Cultivation: Average soil, grow in a 12-inch pot, easily self-seeds

DIY TIP: Add borage flowers to the ritual cup to gladden your heart at Litha. Carry borage for courage. Sprinkle borage on your divination tools to enhance your psychic abilities.

BRACKEN

Pteridium aquilinum

Size: 3 feet

Parts Used: Leaves

Safety Considerations: Toxic for humans and pets.

Planetary Ruler: Mercury

Moon Phase: Waxing

Element: Air

Zodiac Sign: Gemini

Gender: Masculine

Deity: Kupala

Lore: Burning bracken or pulling it up by the roots was said to cause a storm.

Magical Purpose: Healing, rain magic, dreams

MAGICAL AMPLIFIERS

- ◆ **Angel:** Raphael
- ◆ **Chakras:** Third Eye, Heart
- ◆ **Crystals:** Amethyst, moonstone, sodalite
- ◆ **Tarot:** The Sun

FOR FORAGING

Bracken shoots, such as fiddlehead ferns, are considered edible in small amounts but require thorough preparation before consumption due to the carcinogenic compound ptaquiloside. Forage throughout North America in pastures and woodlands. USDA Plant Hardiness Zone 3–11

DIY TIP: Adding fern fronds to spells or flower arrangements will boost their magical properties. Dried bracken fronds make an excellent mulch; when burned, their ashes can be used as a high-potassium fertilizer.

BROMELIAD

Bromeliaceae

Size: 1 inch to 3 feet

Parts Used: Leaves, flowers

Safety Considerations: Nontoxic for humans and pets.

Planetary Ruler: Sun

Moon Phase: Waxing

Element: Air

Zodiac Sign: Leo

Gender: Masculine

Deity: Kupala

Lore: The Aztecs and Mayans viewed bromeliad plants as "gifts from the gods" and used them for food, shelter, clothing, and rituals.

Magical Purpose: Protection, money

MAGICAL AMPLIFIERS

♦ **Angel:** Raphael
♦ **Chakra:** Heart
♦ **Crystals:** Topaz
♦ **Tarot:** The Sun

DIY TIP: Air plants are bromeliads that grow without any soil. They grow on natural tree branches, but you can grow them in glass containers, driftwood, or a simple tray or dish.

FOR GARDENING

Bromeliads have a fantastic array of colors and textures. They are a slow-growing houseplant that will take up to 3 years to mature.

Suggested Varieties for Beginners: Guzmania, Neoregelia

Location: Houseplant

Light: Bright, indirect light

Water and Food: Light watering; some species are watered directly into the central "cup" of the plant; feed with a liquid fertilizer diluted to half-strength monthly

Soil, Pot, Cultivation: Fast-draining potting soil mixed with sand, grow in 3- to 18-inch pots, repot offshoots that appear after the plant flowers

BROOM

Cytisus scoparius

Size: 10 feet

Parts Used: Flowers, branches

Safety Considerations: Toxic for humans and pets. Broom is safe to handle but should not be ingested or applied to the skin.

Planetary Ruler: Moon

Moon Phase: New

Element: Water

Zodiac Sign: Pisces

Gender: Feminine

Deity: Mercury, Morpheus

Lore: The medieval name of broom was *Planta genista*; King Henry II of England used it to create his family name of Plantagenet.

Magical Purpose: Purification, protection, astral travel

MAGICAL AMPLIFIERS

◆ **Angel:** Zadkiel
◆ **Chakra:** Root
◆ **Crystal:** Opal
◆ **Tarot:** Death
◆ **Sacred to:** Samhain

DIY TIP: Gather blooming broom branches in the spring and ritually sweep your house to clear it of negative energy and purify it for the coming summer months.

FOR GARDENING

Broom is safe to handle but should not be ingested or applied to the skin.

Location: USDA Plant Hardiness Zone 5–8

Light: Full sun

Foraging: Forage on the East and West coasts, Idaho, Montana, and Utah; invasive species

BURDOCK

Arctium lappa

Size: 2 to 9 feet

Parts Used: Stems, leaves, seeds, root

Safety Considerations: Edible. Nontoxic for humans and pets.

Planetary Ruler: Venus

Moon Phase: Waning

Element: Water

Zodiac Sign: Cancer

Gender: Feminine

Deity: Gaia

Lore: In folk magic, burdock was called bat weed. It was gathered during a waning Moon and used for cleansing, for warding off negativity, and in protection spells.

Magical Purpose: Protection, healing

MAGICAL AMPLIFIERS

- ♦ **Angel:** Raphael
- ♦ **Chakra:** Heart
- ♦ **Crystals:** Blue lace agate, sodalite, turquoise
- ♦ **Tarot:** The Sun

FOR FORAGING

Burdock is a common biennial weed found throughout North America. Young burdock roots can be roasted and eaten. Forage throughout North America. USDA Plant Hardiness Zone 2–11

DIY TIP: Harvest young leaves in the spring and roots in the fall. Use large burdock leaves to wrap food for campfire cooking.

BUTTERCUP

Ranunculus abortivus

Size: 14 to 16 inches

Parts Used: Flowers

Safety Considerations: Toxic for humans and pets. Never rub the flowers or leaves on your skin; they will cause blistering.

Planetary Ruler: Sun

Moon Phase: Full

Element: Fire

Zodiac Sign: Leo

Gender: Masculine

Deity: Aphrodite

Lore: Buttercups are sacred to fairies, who use them as cups.

Magical Purpose: Love, divination, innocence

MAGICAL AMPLIFIERS

- ◆ **Angel:** Chamuel
- ◆ **Chakra:** Heart
- ◆ **Crystals:** Alexandrite, desert rose, tanzanite
- ◆ **Tarot:** The Lovers

FOR FORAGING

The entire buttercup plant is toxic, so only gather and use it for spells and rituals. Forage throughout North America. USDA Plant Hardiness Zone 8–10

DIY TIP: Buttercups are very hard to grow from seed, so plant from root stock. Buttercup roots may be dug up and divided in the fall.

CARAWAY

Carum carvi

Size: 2 feet

Parts Used: Seeds

Safety Considerations: Edible. Toxic to pets, nontoxic for humans.

Planetary Ruler: Mercury

Moon Phase: Waxing

Element: Air

Zodiac Sign: Gemini

Gender: Masculine

Deity: Persephone

Lore: Caraway seeds were found in the garbage piles of prehistoric communities. German folklore advises placing a dish of the seeds under the bed to protect from witches!

Magical Purpose: Protection, lust, memory, health, anti-theft

MAGICAL AMPLIFIERS

◆ **Angel:** Raphael
◆ **Chakra:** Third Eye
◆ **Crystals:** Amethyst, angelite, celestine, clear quartz
◆ **Tarot:** The Magician

DIY TIP: Make a dream pillow using caraway seeds, mint, and lavender. To protect you from theft, sprinkle seeds in your car and wallet—or any place that needs it.

FOR GARDENING

Caraway looks somewhat like carrot plants. It has a long taproot like a parsnip. Sow seeds directly outdoors in the spring; it does not transplant well.

Suggested Varieties for Beginners: Common caraway

Location: USDA Plant Hardiness Zone 4–10

Light: Full sun to part shade

Water and Food: Regular watering, add compost in spring and balanced fertilizer monthly

Soil, Pot, Cultivation: Sandy, compost-rich soil; plant in pots that are 24 inches deep; self-seeds

THE GREEN WITCH'S HERB AND PLANT ENCYCLOPEDIA

CARNATION

Dianthus caryophyllus

Size: 1 to 2 feet

Parts Used: Flowers

Safety Considerations: Edible. Toxic to pets, nontoxic for humans.

Planetary Ruler: Sun

Moon Phase: Waxing

Element: Fire

Zodiac Sign: Aries, Capricorn, Sagittarius

Gender: Masculine

Deity: Artemis, Diana, Zeus

Lore: When Zeus discovered that Hera had a flower dedicated to her and he didn't, he got so mad that he threw a lightning bolt at Earth that caused a carnation.

Magical Purpose: Authority, beauty, harmony, healing

MAGICAL AMPLIFIERS

- ♦ **Angel:** Michael
- ♦ **Chakra:** Solar Plexus
- ♦ **Crystals:** Amber, citrine, pyrite, tiger's-eye
- ♦ **Tarot:** Temperance

DIY TIP: Carnation color magic
PINK: Friendship
RED: Marriage
WHITE: Innocence
YELLOW: Happiness
ORANGE: Courage

FOR GARDENING

Carnation is fragrant and easy to grow with full sun and well-drained soil.

Suggested Varieties for Beginners: Sweet William, Cheddar pinks

Location: USDA Plant Hardiness Zone 7–10

Light: Full sun

Water and Food: Regular watering, add compost in spring and balanced fertilizer monthly

Soil, Pot, Cultivation: Rich soil with added compost, grow in 12-inch pots, pinch off dead flowers

CATNIP

Nepeta cataria

Size: 2 to 3 feet

Parts Used: Flowers, leaves

Safety Considerations: Edible. Nontoxic for humans and pets.

Planetary Ruler: Venus

Moon Phase: Full

Element: Water

Zodiac Sign: Cancer, Libra, Pisces

Gender: Feminine

Deity: Bast, Sekhmet

Lore: Catnip may have gotten its name from the ancient city of Nepete or Nepeti, where it was grown for teas and herbal remedies.

Magical Purpose: Animal magic, peace, love, beauty, happiness

MAGICAL AMPLIFIERS

- ◆ **Angel:** Gabriel
- ◆ **Chakra:** Heart
- ◆ **Crystals:** Cat's-eye, jasper, labradorite
- ◆ **Tarot:** The Lovers
- ◆ **Sacred to:** Samhain

DIY TIP: To treat colds, flu, and bronchitis, pour a cup of boiling water over 3 tablespoons of catnip, steep for 10 minutes, and drink three times daily.

FOR GARDENING

Catnip has fragrant foliage with spikes of flowers that bloom from late spring to fall.

Suggested Varieties for Beginners: True catnip, Greek catnip

Location: USDA Plant Hardiness Zone 3–9

Light: Full sun to part shade

Water and Food: Regular watering, add compost in spring and balanced fertilizer monthly

Soil, Pot, Cultivation: Average, well-drained soil; grow in 10-inch pots; divide in early spring

CEDAR

Cedrus libani

Size: 40 to 100 feet

Parts Used: Leaves, bark

Safety Considerations: Nontoxic for humans and pets.

Planetary Ruler: Sun

Moon Phase: Waning

Element: Fire

Zodiac Sign: Sagittarius

Gender: Masculine

Deity: Arinna

Lore: Lebanon cedar was used to build King Solomon's temple, and cedarwood oil was one of the first ingredients in ancient perfumery.

Magical Purpose: Healing, purification, protection

MAGICAL AMPLIFIERS

- ◆ **Angel:** Michael
- ◆ **Chakra:** Solar Plexus
- ◆ **Crystals:** Diamond, tiger's-eye, topaz
- ◆ **Tarot:** The Emperor

FOR FORAGING

Lebanon cedar is not native to North America but is grown in the landscape throughout the United States. It is a true cedar and is not to be confused with the typical native North American cedars: Cupressus, Juniperus, and Thuja, which are not cedars at all. Forage with permission from parks and private property. USDA Plant Hardiness Zone 5–9

DIY TIP: Bundle 8-inch trimmed cedar fronds and wrap them tightly with string to create a smoke-cleansing stick.

CHAMOMILE

Chamaemelum nobile

Size: 2 feet

Parts Used: Leaves, flowers

Safety Considerations: Edible. Nontoxic in small amounts for pets; nontoxic for humans.

Planetary Ruler: Sun

Moon Phase: Waxing

Element: Water

Zodiac Sign: Cancer, Leo

Gender: Masculine

Deity: Cernunnos, Ra, Helios

Lore: The Egyptians dedicated chamomile to Ra, the Sun god. Chamomile was one of the herbs mentioned in the ancient Lacuna herbal manuscript.

Magical Purpose: Attraction, blessings, intuition, prosperity, sleep, purification

MAGICAL AMPLIFIERS

- ◆ **Angel:** Michael
- ◆ **Chakra:** Heart
- ◆ **Crystals:** Bloodstone, peridot
- ◆ **Tarot:** The Hermit
- ◆ **Sacred to:** Yule, Litha

DIY TIP: Plant chamomile near sick plants to return them to health. Use chamomile tea to water young plants to prevent "damping off," a fungus that grows on seedlings.

FOR GARDENING

Chamomile has fragrant, feathery foliage with small, daisy-shaped flowers and is a good ground cover.

Suggested Varieties for Beginners: Common chamomile, Roman chamomile

Location: USDA Plant Hardiness Zone 3–9

Light: Full sun to part shade

Water and Food: Regular watering, add compost in spring and balanced fertilizer monthly

Soil, Pot, Cultivation: Average, well-drained soil; any container size; pinch new growth but don't cut into woody stems

CHICORY

Cichorium intybus

Size: 3 to 5 feet

Parts Used: Flowers, stems, leaves, root, seeds

Safety Considerations: Edible. Nontoxic for humans and pets.

Planetary Ruler: Sun

Moon Phase: Waning

Element: Earth

Zodiac Sign: Virgo

Gender: Feminine

Deity: Apollo, Clytia

Lore: Roman legend has it that Chicory was once a beautiful woman beloved by the sun. The sun asked chicory to marry him, but she refused, so he turned her into a plant fated to follow his progress across the sky every day.

Magical Purpose: Faithfulness, pride, penance

MAGICAL AMPLIFIERS

- ◆ **Angel:** Chamuel
- ◆ **Chakra:** Heart
- ◆ **Crystals:** Aquamarine, chalcedony, labradorite
- ◆ **Tarot:** Temperance

FOR FORAGING

Chicory roots can be roasted and ground up to use as a coffee substitute. Young leaves are good in salads. Forage throughout North America. USDA Plant Hardiness Zone 3–8

DIY TIP: To soothe and heal skin inflammations, bruise fresh chicory leaves and apply them to the skin.

CHICKWEED
Stellaria media

Size: 4 inches

Parts Used: Flowers, leaves

Safety Considerations: Edible. In small amounts, nontoxic for humans and pets.

Planetary Ruler: Moon

Moon Phase: Full

Element: Water

Zodiac Sign: Cancer

Gender: Feminine

Deity: Triple Goddess

Lore: Chickweed may have gotten its name because it was a favorite foraging food for chickens. Before the use of limes, sailors ate chickweed on long voyages to prevent scurvy.

Magical Purpose: Fidelity, love

MAGICAL AMPLIFIERS

- ♦ **Angel:** Chamuel
- ♦ **Chakra:** Heart
- ♦ **Crystals:** Rose quartz, amethyst, agate
- ♦ **Tarot:** The Lovers

FOR FORAGING

Chickweed can be eaten raw in salads or cooked like spinach. It has a mild flavor, somewhat like corn silk. Forage throughout North America in lawns, pastures, and waste areas. USDA Plant Hardiness Zone 4–11

DIY TIP: Infuse chickweed in olive oil to treat irritated skin. Add chickweed to footbaths to soothe tired feet.

CHILE PEPPER
Capsicum spp.

Size: 1 to 2 feet

Parts Used: Fruit

Safety Considerations: Edible. Nontoxic in small amounts for pets; nontoxic for humans.

Planetary Ruler: Mars

Moon Phase: Waning, Dark

Element: Fire

Zodiac Sign: Sagittarius

Gender: Masculine

Deity: Mars

Lore: The remains of 9,000-year-old chiles were found in Mexican dig sites. The Inca people revered the chile pepper as a sacred plant.

Magical Purpose: Fidelity, hex-breaking, love

MAGICAL AMPLIFIERS

- ♦ **Angel:** Chamuel
- ♦ **Chakra:** Root
- ♦ **Crystals:** Carnelian, ruby, smoky quartz
- ♦ **Tarot:** The Emperor

DIY TIP: String chile peppers, dry them, and hang them in your kitchen to promote positive energy.

FOR GARDENING

Peppers are attractive and ornamental; they do very well in pots indoors or planted outside when the weather is warm.

Suggested Varieties for Beginners: Caribbean, Long Red Cayenne

Location: USDA Plant Hardiness Zone 9–11; grow as an annual in cooler zones

Light: Full sun

Water and Food: Regular watering, balanced fertilizer twice during the growing season

Soil, Pot, Cultivation: Average soil, grow in 12-inch pots, plant when night temperatures are above 55°F

CHRYSANTHEMUM

Chrysanthemum morifolium

Size: 1 to 3 feet

Parts Used: Flowers, leaves

Safety Considerations: Toxic for humans and pets. All parts of chrysanthemum are toxic if ingested and can cause skin reactions or respiratory issues; always wear gloves when handling this plant.

Planetary Ruler: Sun

Moon Phase: Waning

Element: Fire

Zodiac Sign: Leo

Gender: Masculine

Deity: Izanagi, Iznami

Lore: In many European countries, the chrysanthemum is considered a funeral plant and is only used for burial rites. Ancient Greeks wore garlands of chrysanthemum flowers to banish evil spirits.

Magical Purpose: Protection

MAGICAL AMPLIFIERS

- **Angel:** Michael
- **Chakra:** Solar Plexus
- **Crystals:** Smoky quartz, carnelian, citrine
- **Tarot:** The High Priestess
- **Sacred to:** Mabon, Samhain

FOR GARDENING

Chrysanthemums bloom late in the season and can add a splash of color to your fall garden.

Suggested Varieties for Beginners: Anemone, Pompon

Location: USDA Plant Hardiness Zone 4–9

Light: Full sun

Water and Food: Regular watering, fertilize monthly until July

Soil, Pot, Cultivation: Rich, well-drained soil with organic matter; grow in 8- to 12-inch pots; pinch out half of the new growth every 2 weeks for bushy plants

DIY TIP: Place chrysanthemum flowers on the Samhain altar as an offering to ancestors. Grow chrysanthemum near your front door to protect your home from negative energy.

CINNAMON

Cinnamomum zeylanicum

Size: 4 to 5 feet

Parts Used: Leaves, bark

Safety Considerations: Edible. Nontoxic in small amounts for pets; nontoxic for humans.

Planetary Ruler: Sun

Moon Phase: Waxing

Element: Fire

Zodiac Sign: Aries, Capricorn, Leo

Gender: Masculine

Deity: Venus, Aphrodite

Lore: Ancient Egyptians used cinnamon with other herbs and spices for mummification.

Magical Purpose: Astral realm, clairvoyance, blessing, spirituality, success, healing, protection

MAGICAL AMPLIFIERS

- ◆ **Angel:** Michael
- ◆ **Chakra:** Crown
- ◆ **Crystals:** Amethyst, fluorite, sapphire, sunstone
- ◆ **Tarot:** The Sun

DIY TIP: Burn a cinnamon stick to purify and cleanse your home or sacred space. Create a money-drawing sachet using cinnamon, cloves, nutmeg, and ginger.

FOR GARDENING

Cinnamon has glossy green to yellow-green aromatic foliage.

Suggested Varieties for Beginners: True cinnamon, Chinese cinnamon

Location: USDA Plant Hardiness Zone 10–12; grow as a houseplant in cooler zones

Light: Full sun to part shade

Water and Food: Regular watering, allow the soil to dry out between waterings, fertilize sparingly

Soil, Pot, Cultivation: Prefers acidic potting soil, grow in pots 3 inches larger than the root ball, keep pruned to under 4 feet

CINQUEFOIL

Potentilla

Size: 2 to 4 feet

Parts Used: Leaves, flowers

Safety Considerations: Edible. Nontoxic for humans and pets.

Planetary Ruler: Jupiter

Moon Phase: Full

Element: Fire

Zodiac Sign: Gemini

Gender: Masculine

Deity: Venus

Lore: Cinquefoil flowers have five leaves that are said to represent love, money, health, power, and wisdom. It is often seen at the top of Gothic arches and could be a secret symbol representing the Goddess. In arcane spells, when the ingredients call for "fingers," it means cinquefoil!

Magical Purpose: Money, protection, dreams

MAGICAL AMPLIFIERS

- ◆ **Angel:** Michael
- ◆ **Chakra:** Throat
- ◆ **Crystals:** Opal
- ◆ **Tarot:** Judgment

> **DIY TIP:** In late winter, prune cinquefoil into a rounded shape.

FOR GARDENING

Cinquefoil is a flowering shrub that grows in a mound with bluish-green leaves and five-petaled flowers in white, peach, pink, or yellow.

Suggested Varieties for Beginners: Pink Queen, Snowbird

Location: USDA Plant Hardiness Zone 2–7

Light: Full sun to part shade

Water and Food: Light watering, drought tolerant, fertilize once in early spring

Soil, Pot, Cultivation: Regular well-drained soil; the pot should be 3 inches larger than the root ball; fertilize potted plant monthly

CLOVER

Trifolium spp.

Size: 4 to 6 inches

Parts Used: Flowers, leaves

Safety Considerations: Edible. Nontoxic in small amounts for pets; nontoxic for humans.

Planetary Ruler: Mercury

Moon Phase: New

Element: Air

Zodiac Sign: Gemini

Gender: Masculine

Deity: Gwydion

Lore: Three-leafed clover was associated with the Christian Trinity, and the rarer four-leafed clover was related to the Christian cross.

Magical Purpose: Enchantment, intuition, luck, fairy magic, protection, wealth

MAGICAL AMPLIFIERS

- ♦ **Angel:** Raphael
- ♦ **Chakra:** Heart
- ♦ **Crystals:** Amethyst, opal, rose quartz
- ♦ **Tarot:** Wheel of Fortune

DIY TIP: Place a cloverleaf in your shoe to find a wealthy new lover. White clover helps break hexes, and red clover removes negative energy.

FOR GARDENING

Clover is a low-growing perennial with white or pink flowers and creeping stems.

Suggested Varieties for Beginners: White clover, red clover

Location: USDA Plant Hardiness Zone 1–8

Light: Full sun to part shade

Water and Food: Regular watering, add compost in spring and balanced fertilizer monthly

Soil, Pot, Cultivation: Average soil, grow in pots at least 6 inches wide, can be harvested twice during the growing season

COLUMBINE

Aquilegia

Size: 1 to 3 feet

Parts Used: Flowers, leaves

Safety Considerations: Toxic for humans and pets. Columbine flowers are safe to eat in moderation; the roots and seeds are highly toxic. The plant sap can be irritating, so wear gloves.

Planetary Ruler: Venus

Moon Phase: Waxing

Element: Water

Zodiac Sign: Pisces

Gender: Feminine

Deity: Aphrodite, Freya

Lore: The ancient Celts believed that columbine could open doors to other worlds. *Aquilegia* means "eagle" and refers to the pointed flower petals resembling an eagle's talons.

Magical Purpose: Courage, peace

MAGICAL AMPLIFIERS

- ◆ **Angel:** Gabriel
- ◆ **Chakra:** Solar Plexus
- ◆ **Crystals:** Aquamarine, black tourmaline, tiger's-eye
- ◆ **Tarot:** The Fool

> **DIY TIP:** Columbine is a plant beloved by the fairy folk; when it appears, it means they have blessed your garden.

FOR GARDENING

Columbine flowers are attractive to hummingbirds.

Suggested Varieties for Beginners: Nana, Crimson Star

Location: USDA Plant Hardiness Zone 3–8

Light: Part sun to part shade

Water and Food: Regular watering, mulch in summer, liquid fertilizer twice during the growing season

Soil, Pot, Cultivation: Regular soil; grow in 10-inch pots; avoid hot, full-sun sites

COMFREY

Symphytum

Size: 1 to 3 feet

Parts Used: Flowers, leaves, root

Safety Considerations: Nontoxic in small amounts for humans and pets. Contains dangerous alkaloids.

Planetary Ruler: Saturn

Moon Phase: Waxing

Element: Water

Zodiac Sign: Libra

Gender: Feminine

Deity: Hermes, Mercury

Lore: Comfrey was traditionally used to heal broken skin and bones, so brides-to-be who weren't virgins hoped that sitting in water infused with comfrey would restore their virginity.

Magical Purpose: Safe travel, money

MAGICAL AMPLIFIERS

- ◆ **Angel:** Raphael
- ◆ **Chakra:** Root
- ◆ **Crystals:** Amethyst, celestite, hematite
- ◆ **Tarot:** The World

> **DIY TIP:** Place cut comfrey leaves near your garden to divert slugs away from your plants and dispose of them.

FOR GARDENING

Comfrey is easy to grow and will spread by reseeding. It can be invasive, so remove spent flower heads.

Suggested Varieties for Beginners: Common comfrey

Location: USDA Plant Hardiness Zone 4–8

Light: Full sun to part shade

Water and Food: Regular watering, add compost in the spring

Soil, Pot, Cultivation: Regular soil; not suitable for containers; when plants die back in fall, cover them with mulch

COWSLIP
Primula veris

Size: 8 to 10 inches

Parts Used: Leaves, flowers

Safety Considerations: Nontoxic in small amounts for both humans and pets.

Planetary Ruler: Venus

Moon Phase: Dark, New

Element: Water

Zodiac Sign: Aries, Scorpio

Gender: Feminine

Deity: Freya

Lore: Cowslip is beloved by the fairy folk and is believed to be a passageway to fairyland. Druids carried the flowers to protect them from evil.

Magical Purpose: Youth, fidelity, harmony, grace, secrets, spirit world

MAGICAL AMPLIFIERS
- **Angel:** Gabriel
- **Chakra:** Sacral
- **Crystals:** Moonstone, obsidian, onyx, tourmaline
- **Tarot:** The Moon
- **Sacred to:** Ostara

> **DIY TIP:** Place cowslip flowers on your doorstep to gain fairy blessings.

FOR GARDENING

Cowslip blooms in early to late spring and has flowers borne on individual stems or in clusters above the leaves.

Suggested Varieties for Beginners: Sweetheart, Gemini, Nosegay

Location: USDA Plant Hardiness Zone 1–8

Light: Shade to part shade

Water and Food: Keep moist, add compost in the spring and fertilizer monthly

Soil, Pot, Cultivation: Organic, rich soil; grow in pots at least 6 inches wide; divide clumps after blooming in the spring

CYCLAMEN

Cyclamen

Size: 6 to 9 inches

Parts Used: Flowers, leaves

Safety Considerations: Toxic for humans and pets. All parts of the plant are toxic if ingested and it can cause skin irritation; wear gloves when handling.

Planetary Ruler: Venus

Moon Phase: Full

Element: Water

Zodiac Sign: Scorpio

Gender: Feminine

Deity: Hecate

Lore: Cyclamen derives from the Greek word *kyklaminos*, from *kyklos*, meaning "circle."

Magical Purpose: Fertility, protection, happiness, lust

MAGICAL AMPLIFIERS

◆ **Angel:** Gabriel
◆ **Chakra:** Heart
◆ **Crystals:** Rose quartz, pink kunzite, rhodonite
◆ **Tarot:** The Lovers

> **DIY TIP:** Once cyclamen begins to go dormant, allow it to dry out for 2 to 3 months. Look for new growth at the base and start regular watering again to begin the growth cycle.

FOR GARDENING

Cyclamen is a small tuberous perennial with heart-shaped leaves and flowers that grow on long stems.

Suggested Varieties for Beginners: Sierra, Scentsation

Location: Houseplant

Light: Bright, indirect light

Water and Food: Regular watering, avoid getting water on the leaves; use liquid low-nitrogen fertilizer twice a month

Soil, Pot, Cultivation: Acidic potting mix, the pot should be large enough to leave a 1-inch space around the tuber, cut off dead flower stalks and leaves

DAFFODIL

Narcissus

Size: 6 to 30 inches

Parts Used: Bulb, flower

Safety Considerations: Toxic for humans and pets. All parts of daffodil are toxic if ingested, but the bulb has the highest toxicity concentration. Always wear gloves when handling.

Planetary Ruler: Venus

Moon Phase: Full

Element: Water

Zodiac Sign: Leo

Gender: Feminine

Deity: Persephone

Lore: The Goddess Venus turned Narcissus into a daffodil so he wouldn't starve to death while he was mesmerized by gazing at his reflection.

Magical Purpose: Love, fertility, luck

MAGICAL AMPLIFIERS

- **Angel:** Chamuel
- **Chakra:** Heart
- **Crystals:** Aquamarine, amethyst, rose quartz
- **Tarot:** The Moon
- **Sacred to:** Ostara

> **DIY TIP:** Add red food coloring to the water in a daffodil vase for red-tinged flowers.

FOR GARDENING

Daffodils are among the most popular spring-blooming bulbs.

Suggested Varieties for Beginners: Petit Four, Crewenna

Location: USDA Plant Hardiness Zone 4–8

Light: Full sun to part shade

Water and Food: Regular watering, apply bulb food in spring

Soil, Pot, Cultivation: Rich, moist soil with good drainage; grow in 12- to 18-inch pots; remove the flower and stem after blooming, allow the foliage to die back naturally

DANDELION

Taraxacum officinale

Size: 2 to 24 inches

Parts Used: Leaves, flowers, root

Safety Considerations: Edible. Nontoxic for humans and pets.

Planetary Ruler: Jupiter

Moon Phase: Waxing

Element: Air

Zodiac Sign: Sagittarius

Gender: Masculine

Deity: Hecate, Belenos

Lore: Dandelion's name comes from the French phrase *dent de lion*, which means "tooth of the lion."

Magical Purpose: Divination, wishes, the spirit world

MAGICAL AMPLIFIERS

- **Angel:** Gabriel
- **Chakra:** Throat
- **Crystals:** Celestite, lapis lazuli, clear quartz
- **Tarot:** The Star

FOR FORAGING

Dandelions' cheery bright yellow flowers signal the end of winter and are one of the earliest pollen sources for honeybees. Harvest young blossoms, leaves, and roots anytime. Forage throughout North America. USDA Plant Hardiness Zone 3–9

DIY TIP: Send a message to the spirit world by blowing the seed head toward the North.

DATURA

Datura stramonium

Size: 2 to 4 feet

Parts Used: Leaves, flowers, seeds

Safety Considerations: Poisonous to humans and pets. All parts are deadly poison if ingested; always wear gloves when handling.

Planetary Ruler: Saturn

Moon Phase: Full

Element: Water

Zodiac Sign: Scorpio

Gender: Feminine

Deity: Hecate, Kali

Lore: Datura belongs to the nightshade family; datura, belladonna, henbane, and mandrake are known as the Weird Sisters. During the Spanish Inquisition, growing or using datura and other solanaceous plants could bring an accusation of witchcraft.

Magical Purpose: Astral travel, divination, invisibility, shape-shifting

MAGICAL AMPLIFIERS

- **Angel:** Zadkiel
- **Chakra:** Crown
- **Crystals:** Angelite, fluorite, moonstone
- **Tarot:** The Moon

DIY TIP: The only safe way to use datura to induce visions is by inhaling the flower's scent while it's still on the plant.

FOR GARDENING

Datura has large, trumpet-shaped flowers and grows rapidly.

Suggested Varieties for Beginner: Jimsonweed

Location: USDA Plant Hardiness Zone 5-10

Light: Full sun

Water and Food: Regular watering, fertilize in spring and summer

Soil, Pot, Cultivation: Light, well-drained soil; grow in 10-inch pots; treat as an annual in cooler climates

DILL

Anethum graveolens

Size: 2 to 4 feet

Parts Used: Seeds, leaves

Safety Considerations: Edible. Nontoxic for humans and pets.

Planetary Ruler: Mercury

Moon Phase: Waning

Element: Fire

Zodiac Sign: Cancer, Gemini, Leo, Scorpio, Virgo

Gender: Masculine

Deity: Hecate, Isis

Lore: Dill was used by the Romans, who spread it throughout Europe. It was a common spice used by the Norse and was a popular medieval garden herb.

Magical Purpose: Defense, desire, money, prophecy, willpower

MAGICAL AMPLIFIERS

- ♦ **Angel:** Raphael
- ♦ **Chakra:** Root
- ♦ **Crystals:** Bloodstone, moss agate, smoky quartz, petrified wood
- ♦ **Tarot:** The High Priestess

DIY TIP: Place dill seeds under your pillow to protect against nightmares. If you're overwhelmed, place a vase of fresh dill near to bring calm and increase concentration.

FOR GARDENING

Dill has delicate, aromatic foliage with bright yellow flowers.

Suggested Varieties for Beginners: Bouquet, Greensleeves, Hera

Location: USDA Plant Hardiness Zone 2–11

Light: Full sun

Water and Food: Regular watering, add compost in spring and balanced fertilizer monthly

Soil, Pot, Cultivation: Average soil, grow in 12-inch pots, will easily reseed itself

DOCK

Rumex crispus

Size: 1½ to 4 feet

Parts Used: Leaves, seeds, root

Safety Considerations: Edible. Toxic to pets, nontoxic for humans.

Planetary Ruler: Jupiter

Moon Phase: Waxing

Element: Air

Zodiac Sign: Libra

Gender: Masculine

Deity: Freya, Lakshmi

Lore: In Europe, dock seeds were used in money charms; after soaking them in water, the liquid was sprinkled throughout the shop to bring in customers.

Magical Purpose: Healing, fertility, money

MAGICAL AMPLIFIERS

♦ **Angel:** Raphael
♦ **Chakra:** Sacral
♦ **Crystals:** Carnelian, moss agate, onyx
♦ **Tarot:** The Empress

FOR FORAGING

Pick tender, young leaves before the flower stalks develop. Dock has a lemony flavor that comes from oxalic acid, which can cause kidney stones if consumed in large amounts. Forage throughout North America. USDA Plant Hardiness Zone 4–8

DIY TIP: Harvest dock for eating in the spring; pick the leaves at the center of the plant. Discard the leaf stem if adding dock to salads.

DOGWOOD

Cornus

Size: 15 to 40 feet

Parts Used: Flowers, berries, leaves, wood

Safety Considerations: Nontoxic for humans and pets.

Planetary Ruler: Saturn

Moon Phase: New

Element: Earth

Zodiac Sign: Capricorn

Gender: Masculine

Deity: Saturn, Venus, Hecate

Lore: It was believed that dogwood was used to form crosses for crucifixion; Jesus prevented the dogwood from growing large enough to be used for making crosses again.

Magical Purpose: Wishes, protection

MAGICAL AMPLIFIERS

♦ **Angels:** Raphael, Michael
♦ **Chakra:** Throat
♦ **Crystals:** Black tourmaline, rose quartz, amethyst
♦ **Tarot:** The Magician

FOR FORAGING

Dogwood is native to the eastern United States. Forage in the eastern United States. USDA Plant Hardiness Zone 5–9

DIY TIP: Make a wish come true by catching a drop of dogwood sap on a cloth on the evening of Litha and wishing on it.

ECHINACEA

Echinacea purpurea

Size: 2 to 5 feet

Parts Used: Flowers, root

Safety Considerations: Edible. Nontoxic for humans and pets.

Planetary Ruler: Mars

Moon Phase: Waxing

Element: Earth

Zodiac Sign: Scorpio

Gender: Masculine

Deity: Athena, Cerridwen

Lore: Echinacea's name comes from the Greek word *echinos*, which describes the bristly nature of the flower's seed heads.

Magical Purpose: Strength, prosperity

MAGICAL AMPLIFIERS

- ◆ **Angel:** Michael
- ◆ **Chakra:** Throat
- ◆ **Crystals:** Clear quartz, citrine, tiger's-eye
- ◆ **Tarot:** Temperance

DIY TIP: Grow echinacea as an offering to the spirits that inhabit your land.

FOR GARDENING

Echinacea is a perennial prairie flower that is easy to grow and drought tolerant and blooms until fall. They have very few issues with pests or diseases as long as they aren't overcrowded.

Suggested Varieties for Beginners: Purple coneflower

Location: USDA Plant Hardiness Zone 3–8

Light: Full sun to part shade

Water and Food: Regular watering, add compost in spring

Soil, Pot, Cultivation: Regular well-drained soil, grow in 24-inch pots, deadhead spent flowers

ELDER

Sambucus canadensis

Size: 5 to 12 feet

Parts Used: Leaves, berries, bark

Safety Considerations: Toxic for humans and pets.

Planetary Ruler: Venus, Mercury

Moon Phase: Waxing

Element: Water

Zodiac Sign: Capricorn, Sagittarius

Gender: Feminine

Deity: Freya, Gaia, Dagda

Lore: English and Scandinavian folklore tell of the "Elder Mother," the guardian of elder trees.

Magical Purpose: Exorcism, protection, healing, prosperity

MAGICAL AMPLIFIERS

- ◆ **Angel:** Azrael
- ◆ **Chakra:** Root
- ◆ **Crystals:** Amber, bloodstone
- ◆ **Tarot:** Death
- ◆ **Sacred to:** Beltane, Litha

FOR FORAGING

Red-fruited elderberry fruit is poisonous; blue-black elderberry fruit is edible once cooked. Forage in the northeastern and northwestern United States. USDA Plant Hardiness Zone 3–9

DIY TIP: The leaves, unripe fruit, and root are toxic and contain cyanide. Cooked berries are safe to eat.

FENNEL
Foeniculum vulgare

Size: 6 feet

Parts Used: Leaves, seeds, root

Safety Considerations: Edible. Nontoxic for humans and pets.

Planetary Ruler: Mercury

Moon Phase: Waning

Element: Fire

Zodiac Sign: Aries, Gemini, Virgo

Gender: Masculine

Deity: Dionysus, Adonis, Prometheus

Lore: Fennel grew all over the Mediterranean in ancient times and was spread throughout Europe by the Romans. Followers of Dionysus made a ceremonial wand out of giant fennel, and it was treasured in monasteries because of its healing properties.

Magical Purpose: Home protection, purification, strength, anti-hex

MAGICAL AMPLIFIERS

♦ **Angel:** Raphael
♦ **Chakra:** Solar Plexus
♦ **Crystals:** Agate, chrysocolla, malachite, topaz
♦ **Tarot:** Strength

> **DIY TIP:** Chew fennel seeds to ease hunger pangs and use them in spells to combat cravings.

FOR GARDENING

Fennel is a tall, feathery herb with fine-textured foliage resembling dill.

Suggested Varieties for Beginners: Rhondo, Cantino, Victoria

Location: USDA Plant Hardiness Zone 5–9

Light: Full sun

Water and Food: Regular watering, add compost in spring and balanced fertilizer monthly

Soil, Pot, Cultivation: Light, well-drained soil; use pots that are 14 inches deep; readily reseeds itself

FEVERFEW

Tanacetum parthenium

Size: 9 to 24 inches

Parts Used: Flowers, leaves

Safety Considerations: Nontoxic for humans and pets.

Planetary Ruler: Venus

Moon Phase: Waning

Element: Fire

Zodiac Sign: Sagittarius

Gender: Masculine

Deity: Danu

Lore: In medieval Europe, people planted feverfew around homes to prevent illness from entering.

Magical Purpose: Protection, banishing

MAGICAL AMPLIFIERS

♦ **Angel:** Michael
♦ **Chakra:** Solar Plexus
♦ **Crystals:** Amber, citrine, sardonyx
♦ **Tarot:** Strength

> **DIY TIP:** Feverfew is easy to grow but can be invasive; it will reseed itself if you don't deadhead the flowers. Dry the flower bunches for use in arrangements.

FOR GARDENING

Feverfew is an aromatic perennial chrysanthemum with small, cheery daisylike white flowers. It's been used for centuries as herbal medicine to treat headaches. Bees and other insects don't like the smell and avoid the plant.

Suggested Varieties for Beginners: White Bonnet, Golden Ball

Location: USDA Plant Hardiness Zone 5–10

Light: Full sun

Water and Food: Generous watering, keep roots moist, add compost in the spring

Soil, Pot, Cultivation: Average, well-drained soil; grow in 12-inch pots; cut it down after the first frost

FLAX

Linum usitatissimum

Size: 2 to 3 feet

Parts Used: Seeds, flowers

Safety Considerations: Nontoxic to humans and pets.

Planetary Ruler: Venus

Moon Phase: Waxing

Element: Earth

Zodiac Sign: Taurus

Gender: Feminine

Deity: Freya, Frigg, Hulda

Lore: Linen, made from the flax plant, is the oldest known cloth, going back to around 8000 BCE. Bits of linen clothing and fishnets have been found at a Stone Age site in Switzerland.

Magical Purpose: Money, protection, healing, beauty

MAGICAL AMPLIFIERS

- ◆ **Angel:** Raphael
- ◆ **Chakra:** Brow, Heart
- ◆ **Crystals:** Malachite, aventurine, tiger's-eye
- ◆ **Tarot:** Empress
- ◆ **Sacred to:** Imbolc, Samhain

FOR FORAGING

Wild flax can be foraged throughout North America in arid rocky soil. It has sky-blue flowers that open in the morning in spring and early summer. USDA Plant Hardiness Zone 2–11

DIY TIP: Place flaxseeds in your wallet or shoes to increase wealth. Add to protection sachets and spells, especially those guarding children.

FOXGLOVE

Digitalis

Size: 2 to 5 feet

Parts Used: Flowers, leaves

Safety Considerations: Toxic for humans and pets. All parts are highly toxic; always wear gloves when handling.

Planetary Ruler: Venus

Moon Phase: Full

Element: Water

Zodiac Sign: Taurus

Gender: Feminine

Deity: Flora

Lore: Plant foxglove wherever you wish to attract fairies. It's said that the spots inside the flowers are fairy handprints and that the fairies taught foxes to ring the foxglove bells to warn other foxes of hunters.

Magical Purpose: Enchantment, fairy magic

MAGICAL AMPLIFIERS

- ◆ **Angel:** Michael
- ◆ **Chakra:** Third Eye
- ◆ **Crystals:** Azurite, lapis lazuli, opal
- ◆ **Tarot:** The Magician
- ◆ **Sacred to:** Summer Solstice

> **DIY TIP:** Foxgloves readily self-seed, and the tiny seedlings will appear at the base of the plant in late summer.

FOR GARDENING

Foxglove is a classic cottage garden plant associated with witches and is a favorite flower of the fairy folk.

Suggested Varieties for Beginners: Common foxglove

Location: USDA Plant Hardiness Zone 4–10

Light: Part sun to part shade

Water and Food: Generous watering, add compost in the spring

Soil, Pot, Cultivation: Loamy, moist, well-drained soil; use a pot that is at least 12 inches deep; deadhead spent flower spikes for a second bloom

GALANGAL

Alpinia galanga

Size: 6 feet

Parts Used: Root, flowers, leaves, fruit

Safety Considerations: Edible. Nontoxic for humans and pets.

Planetary Ruler: Mars

Moon Phase: Waxing

Element: Fire

Zodiac Sign: Aries

Gender: Masculine

Deity: Lakshmi

Lore: Galangal root is called Low John in the closed practice of Hoodoo and is used to win court cases, increase power, and protect from curses.

Magical Purpose: Protection, lust, health

MAGICAL AMPLIFIERS

- **Angel:** Michael
- **Chakra:** Sacral
- **Crystals:** Garnet, pyrite, ruby
- **Tarot:** The Universe
- **Sacred to:** Litha

DIY TIP: Galangal fruit is edible and tastes like cardamom.

FOR GARDENING

Galangal is related to ginger and is native to Indonesia and Iran. The root is called a "hand" because it looks like it has fingers. Grow as an annual in cooler climates or as a houseplant.

Location: USDA Plant Hardiness Zone 9–10

Light: Part sun to part shade

Water and Food: Generous watering, fertilize monthly during the growing season

Soil, Pot, Cultivation: Fertile, loamy, well-drained soil; grow in 18-inch pots; mulch plants with straw to keep the soil cool and moist

GARDENIA
Gardenia jasminoides

Size: 5 to 6 feet

Parts Used: Flowers, leaves

Safety Considerations: Toxic to pets, nontoxic for humans.

Planetary Ruler: Moon

Moon Phase: Full

Element: Water

Zodiac Sign: Cancer, Pisces

Gender: Feminine

Deity: Kuan Yin

Lore: The gardenia is sacred to Morpheus, the Greek god of dreams, and it was believed that the flower's scent could transport a person to paradise.

Magical Purpose: Love, peace, spirituality

MAGICAL AMPLIFIERS
- **Angel:** Chamuel
- **Chakra:** Heart
- **Crystals:** Celestite, angelite, blue lace agate
- **Tarot:** Temperance

DIY TIP: Sprinkle coffee grounds around the base of your plant as a great alternative to commercial fertilizer.

FOR GARDENING

Houseplants can be placed outside in the summer in deep shade.

Suggested Varieties for Beginners: Aimee, Buttons

Location: Indoor houseplant; USDA Plant Hardiness Zone 8–11

Light: Bright light with afternoon shade

Water and Food: Regular watering, use an acid-rich fertilizer monthly

Soil, Pot, Cultivation: Acidic, peat moss–based soil; pot size 3 inches larger than the root ball; gardenias won't tolerate temperatures below 60°F

GARLIC

Allium sativum

Size: 18 to 24 inches

Parts Used: Bulb

Safety Considerations: Edible. Toxic to pets, nontoxic for humans.

Planetary Ruler: Mars

Moon Phase: Waning

Element: Fire

Zodiac Sign: Aries

Gender: Masculine

Deity: Hecate

Lore: Garlic cloves were found in Egyptian King Tutankhamun's tomb and have been used medicinally since the building of the pyramids. During the plague, garlic was used to ward off illness and repel evil spirits, spells, and hexes.

Magical Purpose: Anxiety, exorcism, envy, travel protection, banishing

MAGICAL AMPLIFIERS

- ◆ **Angel:** Chamuel
- ◆ **Chakra:** Solar Plexus
- ◆ **Crystals:** Cat's-eye, jet
- ◆ **Tarot:** The Emperor
- ◆ **Sacred to:** Samhain

DIY TIP: Growing garlic near other plants helps protect them against insect pests. Garlic flowers dry well for flower arrangements.

FOR GARDENING

Garlic is a close cousin to chives, leeks, and onions. It has long, flat leaves and is grown as an annual in herb and vegetable gardens.

Suggested Varieties for Beginners: Artichoke, Silverskin

Location: USDA Plant Hardiness Zone 3–9

Light: Full sun

Water and Food: Regular watering, add compost in the spring

Soil, Pot, Cultivation: Rich, well-drained soil; grow in pots at least 8 inches deep; add nitrogen-rich fertilizer monthly

GOLDENROD

Solidago odora, canadensis

Size: 2 to 6 feet

Parts Used: Leaves, flowers

Safety Considerations: Edible. Nontoxic for humans and pets.

Planetary Ruler: Venus

Moon Phase: Waxing

Element: Air

Zodiac Sign: Gemini

Gender: Feminine

Deity: Sif

Lore: If goldenrod grows near your home, you'll have good luck. Goldenrod was created by a fairy princess who sprinkled gold dust on a stick.

Magical Purpose: Money, divination

MAGICAL AMPLIFIERS

◆ **Angel:** Gabriel

◆ **Chakra:** Root

◆ **Crystals:** Jade, malachite, peridot

◆ **Tarot:** The Sun

DIY TIP: To use goldenrod for dowsing, visualize what you're looking for while holding a sprig in your hands. It will indicate which way to go by nodding.

FOR FORAGING

Young goldenrod leaves are edible; when dried and powdered, crushed leaves can be used to stop bleeding. Forage throughout North America. USDA Plant Hardiness Zone 4–10

GRAPE

Vitis vinifera

Size: 80 feet, unpruned

Parts Used: Leaves, fruit

Safety Considerations: Edible. Toxic to pets, nontoxic for humans.

Planetary Ruler: Moon

Moon Phase: Full

Element: Water

Zodiac Sign: Taurus

Gender: Feminine

Deity: Bacchus, Dionysus, Hathor, Selene

Lore: Grape cultivation is as old as civilization; grapes were mentioned in the Bible and books by Homer. Dionysus is often shown holding a bunch of grapes.

Magical Purpose: Abundance, fertility, garden spells, inspiration, transformation

MAGICAL AMPLIFIERS

- ◆ **Angel:** Gabriel
- ◆ **Chakra:** Root
- ◆ **Crystals:** Aquamarine, tiger's-eye
- ◆ **Tarot:** The Empress
- ◆ **Sacred to:** Mabon

DIY TIP: Harvest grapevines in the winter and weave them into a wreath. Place the wreath in your kitchen to promote abundance.

FOR GARDENING

Grapevines are prolific growers and will need a trellis or arbor for support.

Suggested Varieties for Beginners: Concord, Niagara

Location: USDA Plant Hardiness Zone 4–10

Light: Full sun

Water and Food: Regular watering, fertilize in spring and once more before midsummer

Soil, Pot, Cultivation: Deep, fertile soil; use pots that are 24 inches wide and 18 inches deep; prune judiciously in winter

HAWTHORN

Crataegus

Size: 30 feet

Parts Used: Flowers, leaves, fruit

Safety Considerations: Edible if seeds removed. Nontoxic in small amounts for pets; nontoxic for humans.

Planetary Ruler: Mars

Moon Phase: Full

Element: Fire

Zodiac Sign: Aries

Gender: Masculine

Deity: Flora, Maia

Lore: In Gaelic folklore, hawthorn is associated with fairies and is thought to mark the entrance to the Underworld. The Beltane maypole is traditionally made of hawthorn. It's advisable to ask the fairy's permission before picking the flowers or fruit.

Magical Purpose: Fertility, chastity, happiness

MAGICAL AMPLIFIERS

- **Angel:** Gabriel
- **Chakra:** Sacral
- **Crystals:** Aventurine, selenite, garnet
- **Tarot:** The Moon
- **Sacred to:** Beltane

FOR FORAGING

The raw berries are sweetly tart, but avoid eating the seeds, which contain cyanide. Cooked berries are good in pies, jams, and syrups. Tea can be made with dried flowers, leaves, and berries. Forage throughout North America. USDA Plant Hardiness Zone 5–9

DIY TIP: A tea made of hawthorn bark can be used as a sedative and help regulate blood pressure.

HAZEL

Corylus americana, cornuta

Size: 15 to 18 feet

Parts Used: Leaves, catkins, bark, nuts

Safety Considerations: Edible. Nontoxic for humans and pets.

Planetary Ruler: Sun

Moon Phase: Waxing

Element: Air

Zodiac Sign: Gemini

Gender: Masculine

Deity: Mercury, Thor, Artemis, Diana

Lore: Hazel is sacred to fairies, elves, and garden spirits. Make a wand from a hazel twig and use it to summon them.

Magical Purpose: Luck, fertility, protection, wishes

MAGICAL AMPLIFIERS

- ◆ **Angel:** Michael
- ◆ **Chakra:** Sacral
- ◆ **Crystals:** Amazonite, citrine, garnet
- ◆ **Tarot:** The High Priestess

FOR FORAGING

The nuts are the only edible part of the hazel tree. Pick hazelnuts when the involucre (the protective leafy structure around the nuts) is still green. Forage throughout North America. USDA Plant Hardiness Zone 4-9

DIY TIP: Hazel is at its magical peak after sunset on Samhain, so wait until then to harvest it!

HEATHER

Calluna vulgaris

Size: 18 inches

Parts Used: Stems, flowers

Safety Considerations: Nontoxic for humans and pets.

Planetary Ruler: Mercury

Moon Phase: Waxing

Element: Water

Zodiac Sign: Gemini

Gender: Feminine

Deity: Isis, Osiris

Lore: The Victorians believed that white heather was lucky and that no Scotsman would pass it by without picking some. Fairy lore says that white heather grows over fairy gravesites.

Magical Purpose: Protection, rainmaking, luck

MAGICAL AMPLIFIERS

♦ **Angel:** Jophiel
♦ **Chakra:** Solar Plexus
♦ **Crystals:** Citrine, clear quartz, jade
♦ **Tarot:** Wheel of Fortune
♦ **Sacred to:** Litha

> **DIY TIP:** To bring rain, burn dried heather and fern.

FOR GARDENING

Heather is a small evergreen, woody perennial with tiny flowers that are mauve, purple, or white. There are more than 500 varieties of heather that differ in size, color, and bloom time. Dwarf heather is best for containers.

Suggested Varieties for Beginners: Firefly, Wickwar Flame

Location: USDA Plant Hardiness Zone 4–8

Light: Full sun

Water and Food: Regular watering, fertilizer not required

Soil, Pot, Cultivation: Sandy, acidic soil; grow in 12-inch pots; trim in the spring and after blooming

HELIOTROPE
Heliotropium

Size: 1 to 3 feet

Parts Used: Flowers

Safety Considerations: Toxic for humans and pets. Heliotrope is only toxic if ingested in large amounts and can be safely handled without gloves.

Planetary Ruler: Sun

Moon Phase: Waning

Element: Fire

Zodiac Sign: Leo

Gender: Masculine

Deity: Apollo, Helios

Lore: The name *heliotrope* comes from the Greek words for "sun" (*helios*) and "to turn" (*trepein*), referring to the plant's tendency to face the sun. Place heliotrope flowers under your pillow to dream of lost people or objects.

Magical Purpose: Exorcism, dreams, invisibility

MAGICAL AMPLIFIERS

♦ **Angel:** Zadkiel
♦ **Chakra:** Third Eye
♦ **Crystals:** Amethyst, bloodstone, fluorite
♦ **Tarot:** The Moon
♦ **Sacred to:** Litha

DIY TIP: Heliotrope can be potted up and brought inside as a houseplant over winter.

FOR GARDENING

Heliotrope is a perennial plant that is usually grown as an annual. It has a beautiful vanilla scent and clusters of deep purple flowers.

Suggested Varieties for Beginners: Fragrant Blue, Marine heliotrope

Location: USDA Plant Hardiness Zone 9–11

Light: Full sun to part shade, protect from the hot afternoon sun

Water and Food: Generous watering, fertilize monthly

Soil, Pot, Cultivation: Regular soil, grow in 12-inch pots, pinch and deadhead regularly

HELLEBORE

Helleborus

Size: 1 to 2 feet

Parts Used: Leaves, flowers, seeds, root

Safety Considerations: Poisonous to humans and pets. All parts are deadly poison if ingested; always wear gloves when handling.

Planetary Ruler: Saturn, Mars

Moon Phase: Full

Element: Water

Zodiac Sign: Pisces

Gender: Feminine

Deity: Hecate, Cerridwen

Lore: Hellebore is mentioned in medieval grimoires and is a traditional plant in the witch's garden.

Magical Purpose: Banishing, exorcism, hexing, spirit work

MAGICAL AMPLIFIERS

- ◆ **Angel:** Gabriel
- ◆ **Chakra:** Crown
- ◆ **Crystals:** Selenite, moonstone, opal
- ◆ **Tarot:** The Moon

DIY TIP: To harvest hellebore magically, gather it at midnight while invoking Hecate or Cerridwen.

FOR GARDENING

Hellebore grows easily in shady spots and blooms in midwinter. Be sure to provide shelter from harsh winter winds.

Suggested Varieties for Beginners: Winter Jewels, Angel Glow

Location: USDA Plant Hardiness Zone 3–9

Light: Shade in summer, sun in winter

Water and Food: Generous watering, add compost in the spring

Soil, Pot, Cultivation: Well-drained, rich soil; grow in 14-inch pots; cut back to new growth in the winter if the plant looks scraggly

HENBANE

Hyoscyamus niger

Size: 2 to 4 feet

Parts Used: Flowers, seeds

Safety Considerations: Poisonous to humans and pets. All parts are deadly poison if ingested; always wear gloves when handling.

Planetary Ruler: Saturn

Moon Phase: Waning

Element: Earth

Zodiac Sign: Aquarius

Gender: Feminine

Deity: Belenos, The Morrigan

Lore: The Celts called henbane "beleno," and they burned it in honor of their oracle god Belenus. A German goddess named Bil is called the Fairy of Henbane. She presides over the Rainbow Bridge that connects the earthly and spirit worlds.

Magical Purpose: Astral travel, binding, consecration

MAGICAL AMPLIFIERS

- ◆ **Angel:** Zadkiel
- ◆ **Chakra:** Root
- ◆ **Crystals:** Carnelian, hematite, obsidian
- ◆ **Tarot:** The Fool

FOR GARDENING

Henbane is in the nightshade family and a sister to belladonna and datura. It has attractive flowers with an unpleasant "fishy" odor.

Suggested Varieties for Beginners: Black henbane

Location: USDA Plant Hardiness Zone 4–8

Light: Full sun to part shade

Water and Food: Light watering, add compost in the spring

Soil, Pot, Cultivation: Regular soil, grow in 14-inch pots, has a brittle taproot and doesn't transplant well

DIY TIP: Consecrate ritual tools using water infused with henbane flowers. When the plant is in full bloom, harvest leaves and flowers and collect seeds before the pods open.

HOLLY

Ilex opaca

Size: 40 to 50 feet

Parts Used: Leaves, fruit, wood

Safety Considerations: Poisonous to pets, toxic for humans.

Planetary Ruler: Mars

Moon Phase: Waning

Element: Fire

Zodiac Sign: Aries

Gender: Masculine

Deity: Lugh, Thor

Lore: There will be a hard winter if the holly produces lots of berries.

Magical Purpose: Protection, dreams, anti-lightning

MAGICAL AMPLIFIERS

- ♦ **Angel:** Michael
- ♦ **Chakras:** Root, Heart
- ♦ **Crystals:** Ruby, bloodstone
- ♦ **Tarot:** The Moon
- ♦ **Sacred to:** Lammas, Lughnasadh

DIY TIP: Flowers and berries grow on new wood; prune to promote new growth.

FOR FORAGING

Holly berries are toxic and should never be consumed; holly leaves and branches are nontoxic. If you have young children, remove the berries before bringing boughs into the home. Forage in the southeastern United States. USDA Plant Hardiness Zone 3–9

HONESTY

Lunaria

Size: 2 to 3 feet

Parts Used: Seedpods

Safety Considerations: Nontoxic for humans and pets.

Planetary Ruler: Moon

Moon Phase: Full

Element: Earth

Zodiac Sign: Cancer

Gender: Feminine

Deity: Jupiter, Juno, Io

Lore: To protect his lover from his wife Juno's persecution, Jupiter had the Earth turn Io into a lunaria plant.

Magical Purpose: Money

MAGICAL AMPLIFIERS

- ♦ **Angel:** Gabriel
- ♦ **Chakra:** Third Eye
- ♦ **Crystals:** Moonstone, peridot, quartz
- ♦ **Tarot:** The Sun

DIY TIP: Honesty has purple flowers in the spring that transform into shimmering, coin-shaped seedpods used in money spells.

FOR GARDENING

Honesty or money plants spread quickly by seed; check to see if they are considered invasive where you live. To dry, cut the plants down at the base, bundle the branches with twine, and hang upside down for a few weeks.

Location: USDA Plant Hardiness Zone 4–8

Light: Full sun to part shade

Water and Food: Generous watering, feed once in the spring with slow-release fertilizer

Soil, Pot, Cultivation: Well-drained. humus-rich soil; use a deep pot to accommodate its long taproot; grow from seed

HONEYSUCKLE

Lonicera japonica

Size: 3 to 10 feet

Parts Used: Flowers

Safety Considerations: Edible. Toxic to pets, nontoxic for humans.

Planetary Ruler: Jupiter, Mercury

Moon Phase: Full

Element: Earth

Zodiac Sign: Aries, Cancer, Capricorn, Leo, Pisces, Sagittarius, Scorpio, Taurus, Virgo

Gender: Masculine

Deity: Cerridwen, Gaia, The Morrigan

Lore: During the Bronze Age, honeysuckle stems were used to make rope and are still used in Britain to make harnesses for ponies.

Magical Purpose: Adaptability, attraction, generosity, angel magic, prosperity

MAGICAL AMPLIFIERS

- ◆ **Angel:** Raphael
- ◆ **Chakras:** All
- ◆ **Crystals:** Cat's-eye, jet
- ◆ **Tarot:** Justice
- ◆ **Sacred to:** Beltane, Ostara

DIY TIP: Twine a wreath of honeysuckle around a white candle to invoke the presence of angels.

FOR GARDENING

Honeysuckle is native across North America and Eurasia. Plants are relatively pest-free.

Suggested Varieties for Beginners: Venus Trumpet, Japanese, winter

Location: USDA Plant Hardiness Zone 4–9

Light: Full sun to part shade

Water and Food: Regular watering, add compost in spring and balanced fertilizer monthly

Soil, Pot, Cultivation: Average soil with added compost; grow in an 18-inch pot; train on a trellis, do not prune

HOREHOUND
Marrubium vulgare

Size: 1 to 3 feet

Parts Used: Leaves, flowers

Safety Considerations: Edible. For humans, nontoxic in small amounts; for pets, toxic.

Planetary Ruler: Mercury

Moon Phase: Waning, New

Element: Air, Earth

Zodiac Sign: Gemini, Scorpio, Virgo

Gender: Masculine

Deity: Horus

Lore: Horehound was named after Horus, the god of light and sky, and has been found in ancient Egyptian medicine boxes. Caesar used it as an antidote for poison.

Magical Purpose: Banishing, protection, mental powers, cleansing

MAGICAL AMPLIFIERS
- **Angel:** Raphael
- **Chakra:** Sacral
- **Crystals:** Beryl, jasper, pyrite, serpentine
- **Tarot:** The Magician

FOR GARDENING

Also called white horehound, this plant is drought tolerant and isn't fussy about soil.

Location: USDA Plant Hardiness Zone 3-9

Light: Full sun

Water and Food: Light to regular watering, fertilize once a year

Soil, Pot, Cultivation: Will grow in any well-drained soil, can be invasive, protect from cold and wind

DIY TIP: Bless your home or workspace by leaving out a bowl of water filled with fresh horehound leaves.

HORSETAIL

Equisetum arvense

Size: 20 inches

Parts Used: Leaves, stalk

Safety Considerations: Nontoxic for humans and pets.

Planetary Ruler: Saturn

Moon Phase: Full

Element: Earth

Zodiac Sign: Taurus

Gender: Feminine

Deity: Luna

Lore: Horsetail is a living fossil related to larger plants that grew 270 million years ago. Ancient Greeks used horsetail to heal wounds and treat ulcers.

Magical Purpose: Fertility

MAGICAL AMPLIFIERS

- ♦ **Angel:** Chamuel
- ♦ **Chakra:** Sacral
- ♦ **Crystals:** Aventurine, selenite, unakite
- ♦ **Tarot:** The Moon

> **DIY TIP:** The rough stems are used as sandpaper or to scour pots and pans.

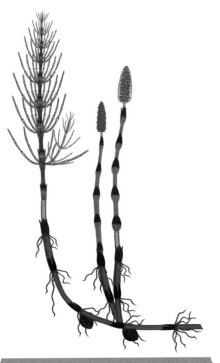

FOR FORAGING

Horsetail spreads by underground rhizomes and spores. Horsetail is a vigorous grower and should only be grown in containers. Forage throughout North America. USDA Plant Hardiness Zone 4–9

HYDRANGEA

Hydrangea

Size: 3 to 15 feet

Parts Used: Flowers

Safety Considerations: Toxic for humans and pets. All parts of hydrangea are toxic if ingested; always wear gloves when handling.

Planetary Ruler: Moon, Jupiter, Neptune

Moon Phase: Full

Element: Water

Zodiac Sign: Scorpio

Gender: Feminine

Lore: The oldest hydrangea fossils were discovered in North America; hydrangea was introduced to Europe in the eighteenth century by North American colonists.

Magical Purpose: Hex-breaking, love, psychic powers

MAGICAL AMPLIFIERS

- **Angel:** Gabriel
- **Chakra:** Heart
- **Crystals:** Clear quartz, moonstone, pearl
- **Tarot:** The Moon

DIY TIP: You can change the color of hydrangea flowers by increasing or decreasing the soil's acidity. Blue flowers are high acidity; pink flowers are low acidity.

FOR GARDENING

Hydrangeas are fast-growing deciduous ornamental shrubs with showy flowers in various colors.

Suggested Varieties for Beginners: Lacecap hydrangea

Location: USDA Plant Hardiness Zone 5–9

Light: Full sun to part shade, protect from the hot afternoon sun

Water and Food: Regular to generous watering, fertilize once in the spring

Soil, Pot, Cultivation: Fertile, humus-rich soil; grow in 24-inch pots; container-grown hydrangeas need winter protection

IVY

Hedera helix

Size: 90 feet

Parts Used: Leaves, stems

Safety Considerations: Toxic for humans and pets.

Planetary Ruler: Saturn

Moon Phase: Waning

Element: Water

Zodiac Sign: Scorpio

Gender: Feminine

Deity: Artemis, Arianrhod, Dionysus

Lore: Ivy grows in a spiral and symbolizes the Goddess. If you dream of ivy, happiness is in your future.

Magical Purpose: Fidelity, prophecy

MAGICAL AMPLIFIERS

- ◆ **Angel:** Gabriel
- ◆ **Chakra:** Third Eye
- ◆ **Crystals:** Obsidian, sodalite, lapis lazuli
- ◆ **Tarot:** The Hanged Man

FOR GARDENING

Ivy leaves and berries are poisonous if consumed, and handling may cause skin irritation; wearing gloves is recommended. Forage throughout North America. USDA Plant Hardiness Zone 4–13

DIY TIP: Plant a pot of ivy and place it wherever protection is needed. Ivy also grows well in a vase of water.

JASMINE

Jasminum

Size: 4 to 30 feet

Parts Used: Flowers, leaves

Safety Considerations: Nontoxic for humans and pets.

Planetary Ruler: Moon

Moon Phase: Full

Element: Water

Zodiac Sign: Pisces

Gender: Feminine

Deity: Tara

Lore: Jasmine is placed in temples and churches to symbolize faith. White jasmine is often used in wedding bouquets and memorial wreaths because of its association with the angelic realm, innocence, and new beginnings.

Magical Purpose: Love, purity, inspiration

MAGICAL AMPLIFIERS

- ♦ **Angel:** Gabriel
- ♦ **Chakra:** Third Eye
- ♦ **Crystals:** Diamond, moonstone, pearl
- ♦ **Tarot:** The High Priestess

DIY TIP: Offer jasmine flowers to Moon goddesses. Only the *Jasminum sambac* is edible.

FOR GARDENING

There are more than 200 different species of jasmine. They are easy to care for, and most are very fragrant.

Suggested Varieties for Beginners: Common jasmine

Location: USDA Plant Hardiness Zone 7–10

Light: Full sun to part shade

Water and Food: Regular watering; don't fertilize until the plant is established, then feed with a slow-release fertilizer in spring and summer

Soil, Pot, Cultivation: Regular soil, use a pot that is 3 inches larger than the root ball, prune only to keep its shape and to remove dead branches

JUNIPER

Juniperus communis

Size: 1 to 15 feet

Parts Used: Leaves, wood, berries

Safety Considerations: For humans, nontoxic in small amounts; for pets, toxic.

Planetary Ruler: Sun

Moon Phase: Waning

Element: Fire

Zodiac Sign: Sagittarius

Gender: Masculine

Deity: Astarte

Lore: Juniper wood was burned to purify temples, contact the spirit world, and enhance clairvoyance.

Magical Purpose: Protection, anti-theft, love, exorcism, health

MAGICAL AMPLIFIERS

- ◆ **Angel:** Michael
- ◆ **Chakra:** Root
- ◆ **Crystals:** Peridot, smoky quartz, jet
- ◆ **Tarot:** The Emperor
- ◆ **Sacred to:** Samhain

FOR FORAGING

Juniper berries are slightly toxic and should be consumed with care. Forage throughout North America. USDA Plant Hardiness Zone 2-9

DIY TIP: Place juniper on the Samhain altar and burn the dried leaves to honor the ancestors.

LADY'S MANTLE

Alchemilla

Size: 12 to 24 inches

Parts Used: Flowers, leaves

Safety Considerations: Nontoxic for humans and pets.

Planetary Ruler: Venus

Moon Phase: Full

Element: Water

Zodiac Sign: Scorpio

Gender: Feminine

Deity: Gaia

Lore: *Alchemilla* means "little alchemist" because lady's mantle was alchemists' favorite magic healing plant. The ancients believed that dew collected from the leaves could purify and cleanse the body of any illness.

Magical Purpose: Love

MAGICAL AMPLIFIERS

- ◆ **Angel:** Gabriel
- ◆ **Chakra:** Heart
- ◆ **Crystals:** Aventurine, emerald, sugilite
- ◆ **Tarot:** Temperance

> **DIY TIP:** Lady's mantle is an excellent contrast for daylilies or paired with plants that have pink or purple foliage or flowers.

FOR GARDENING

Lady's mantle is a charming cottage perennial with interesting leaves and chartreuse flower clusters. Considered invasive in the Pacific Northwest.

Suggested Varieties for Beginners: Irish Silk, Robusta

Location: USDA Plant Hardiness Zone 3–8

Light: Full sun to part shade

Water and Food: Regular watering, drought tolerant once established, fertilizer not required

Soil, Pot, Cultivation: Regular soil; grow in 12-inch pots; deadhead the flowers before they go to seed, shear back in summer if plants begin to look shabby

LAVENDER

Lavender angustifolia

Size: 1 to 3 feet

Parts Used: Flowers, leaves, stems

Safety Considerations: Edible. Nontoxic in small amounts for pets; nontoxic for humans.

Planetary Ruler: Mercury

Moon Phase: Waxing

Element: Air

Zodiac Sign: Aquarius, Gemini, Leo, Pisces, Virgo

Gender: Masculine

Deity: Hecate, Vesta, Saturn

Lore: The Egyptians used lavender in their funeral rites, and King Solomon used it to sprinkle blessed water to cleanse temples.

Magical Purpose: Love, attraction, sleep, longevity, wishes, protection

MAGICAL AMPLIFIERS

- ◆ **Angel:** Raphael
- ◆ **Chakra:** Heart
- ◆ **Crystals:** Jade, topaz
- ◆ **Tarot:** The Hermit
- ◆ **Sacred to:** Summer Solstice, fairies

DIY TIP: Harvest the flowers in the morning once the dew has dried for the best fragrance.

FOR GARDENING

To grow lavender successfully, be sure it's planted in well-drained soil and gets plenty of sunlight.

Suggested Varieties for Beginners: Hidcote, Nana Alba

Location: USDA Plant Hardiness Zone 4–9

Light: Full sun

Water and Food: Light to regular watering, add compost at the beginning of the growing season

Soil, Pot, Cultivation: Poor, well-drained soil; grow in pots more than 8 inches wide; prune in early spring and again in the fall

LEMON BALM

Melissa officinalis

Size: 3 feet

Parts Used: Flowers, leaves

Safety Considerations: Edible. Nontoxic for humans and pets.

Planetary Ruler: Moon, Venus

Moon Phase: Full

Element: Water

Zodiac Sign: Cancer

Gender: Feminine

Deity: Aphrodite

Lore: *Melissa* comes from the Greek word for *honeybee* and was used to attract bees to hives. Paracelsus believed that lemon balm could heal any part of the body. King Charles V drank the healing tea every day.

Magical Purpose: Love, healing, calm

MAGICAL AMPLIFIERS

- **Angel:** Gabriel
- **Chakra:** Heart
- **Crystals:** Peridot, blue lace agate, celestite, moonstone, moss agate
- **Tarot:** The High Priestess

DIY TIP: Make a wreath of fresh lemon balm branches to hang in your home to promote love and friendship.

FOR GARDENING

Lemon balm is easy to grow. It prefers fertile, moist soil and protection from the hot midday sun.

Suggested Varieties for Beginners: Lemon balm

Location: USDA Plant Hardiness Zone 4–9

Light: Part shade to full sun

Water and Food: Regular watering, don't fertilize

Soil, Pot, Cultivation: Moist soil with good drainage, grow in 18-inch pots, divide plants in spring or fall

LILAC

Syringa vulgaris

Size: 12 to 15 feet

Parts Used: Flowers

Safety Considerations: Edible. Nontoxic in small amounts for pets; nontoxic for humans.

Planetary Ruler: Venus

Moon Phase: Full

Element: Water

Zodiac Sign: Libra, Taurus

Gender: Feminine

Deity: Pan

Lore: In Greek mythology, the god Pan pursued a nymph named Syringa, who turned herself into a lilac bush to hide from him.

Magical Purpose: Exorcism, protection, spirit world

MAGICAL AMPLIFIERS

- **Angel:** Gabriel
- **Chakra:** Crown
- **Crystals:** Amethyst, blue lace agate, sodalite
- **Tarot:** The Empress
- **Sacred to:** Beltane

DIY TIP: Mix fresh lilac flowers in yogurt or use them as a pretty cake garnish.

FOR GARDENING

Lilac is easy to grow and can live for more than 100 years. Lilacs won't bloom if they're overfertilized.

Suggested Varieties for Beginners: Congo, Angel White, Charles Joly

Location: USDA Plant Hardiness Zone 3-7

Light: Full sun to part shade

Water and Food: Regular watering, add compost and balanced fertilizer once in early spring

Soil, Pot, Cultivation: Will grow well in all soils if it's not acidic; planting in pots is possible but not ideal; remove spent flowers after blooming

LILY
Lilium

Size: 2 to 4 feet

Parts Used: Flowers

Safety Considerations: Toxic for humans and pets; extremely poisonous to cats. All parts of the lily are toxic if ingested; always wear gloves when handling.

Planetary Ruler: Moon

Moon Phase: Waning

Element: Water

Zodiac Sign: Cancer

Gender: Feminine

Deity: Venus, Juno

Lore: Sweet-scented lilies have long been a symbol of femininity. Greek and Roman brides wore garlands of lilies in their hair to bring them a pure and fruitful married life.

Magical Purpose: Love, purity

MAGICAL AMPLIFIERS
- **Angel:** Gabriel
- **Chakra:** Heart
- **Crystals:** Aquamarine, clear quartz, moonstone
- **Tarot:** The High Priestess
- **Sacred to:** Ostara

DIY TIP: Lily bulbs don't go dormant, so purchase them close to planting time, or the bulbs will deteriorate.

FOR GARDENING

Lily is a perennial flower that blooms from spring to fall, depending on the variety.

Suggested Varieties for Beginners: Asiatic lily, trumpet lily

Location: USDA Plant Hardiness Zone 4–9

Light: Full sun to part sun

Water and Food: Regular watering, add compost in spring and high potassium fertilizer bimonthly

Soil, Pot, Cultivation: Compost-enriched soil that is well-drained and on the acidic side, grow in 16-inch pots, mulch to keep roots cool

LOVAGE

Levisticum officinale

Size: 3 to 6 feet

Parts Used: All parts

Safety Considerations: Edible. Toxic to pets, nontoxic for humans.

Planetary Ruler: Sun

Moon Phase: Waxing

Element: Fire

Zodiac Sign: Pisces, Taurus

Gender: Masculine

Deity: Lofn

Lore: The Romans introduced lovage to the rest of Europe, where it was used for cooking and medicinal purposes. It was brought to America by the British.

Magical Purpose: Attraction, love, omens, purification

MAGICAL AMPLIFIERS

- ♦ **Angel:** Michael
- ♦ **Chakras:** Root, Third Eye
- ♦ **Crystals:** Amethyst, rose quartz
- ♦ **Tarot:** The High Priest

DIY TIP: Use crystallized leaves for decorating cakes, add seeds to salads and bread, and add chopped stems to soups and stews.

FOR GARDENING

Lovage is easy to grow; it prefers moist soil with mulch around the base.

Suggested Varieties for Beginners: Garden lovage

Location: USDA Plant Hardiness Zone 3–9

Light: Full sun to part shade

Water and Food: Regular watering, add compost twice yearly, fertilize once during the growing season

Soil, Pot, Cultivation: Fertile, loamy soil; grow in pots 12 inches deep and wide; harvest leaves before the plant flowers

MAGNOLIA
Magnolia

Size: 5 to 80 feet

Parts Used: Flowers, bark

Safety Considerations: Nontoxic for humans and pets.

Planetary Ruler: Venus

Moon Phase: Waning

Element: Earth

Zodiac Sign: Virgo

Gender: Feminine

Deity: Flora

Lore: Magnolia fossils have been discovered that are 20 million years old; beetles fertilized the flowers because bees had not yet evolved on Earth.

Magical Purpose: Fidelity, longevity

MAGICAL AMPLIFIERS

♦ **Angel:** Uriel
♦ **Chakra:** Solar Plexus
♦ **Crystals:** Iris agate, lodestone, rose quartz
♦ **Tarot:** The Tower

> **DIY TIP:** Magnolia color magic
> **PINK:** Innocence
> **GREEN:** Luck
> **PURPLE:** Health
> **WHITE:** Purity

FOR GARDENING

Magnolia has magnificent, fragrant flowers and can be evergreen or deciduous depending on where it grows.

Suggested Varieties for Beginners: Saucer magnolia

Location: USDA Plant Hardiness Zone 3–9

Light: Full sun to part shade

Water and Food: Regular watering, fertilize sparingly

Soil, Pot, Cultivation: Well-drained, acidic soil with organic matter; use a pot 3 inches larger than the root ball; add peat moss or pine straw to increase acidity

MAIDENHAIR FERN

Adiantum aleuticum

Size: 1 to 3 feet

Parts Used: Leaves

Safety Considerations: Edible. Nontoxic for humans and pets.

Planetary Ruler: Mercury

Moon Phase: Waxing

Element: Earth

Zodiac Sign: Taurus

Gender: Feminine

Deity: Haumea

Lore: Elves and pixies shelter in ferns; whisper your secret wishes to them, and they will be carried to the gods on the four winds.

Magical Purpose: Healing, purity, rain magic

MAGICAL AMPLIFIERS

♦ **Angel:** Ariel
♦ **Chakra:** Crown
♦ **Crystals:** Clear quartz, moonstone, tiger's-eye
♦ **Tarot:** The World
♦ **Sacred to:** Mabon

FOR FORAGING

Fresh fern fronds can be used as a garnish, and dried fronds make a refreshing tea to help treat coughs and bronchitis. Forage throughout North America. USDA Plant Hardiness Zone 3–8

DIY TIP: To collect fern spores, look for fronds with blackish, raised dots on the underside. Place a piece of the frond in an envelope and place it in a warm, dry place for a few days.

MALLOW

Malva sylvestris

Size: 3 to 8 feet

Parts Used: Leaves, flowers, root, seeds

Safety Considerations: Edible. Toxic to pets, nontoxic for humans.

Planetary Ruler: Moon

Moon Phase: Full

Element: Water

Zodiac Sign: Scorpio, Pisces

Gender: Feminine

Deity: Osiris, Althea, Venus, Aphrodite, Shiva

Lore: The ancient Greeks planted mallow at gravesites, and the Romans and the Egyptians ate it as a vegetable.

Magical Purpose: Love, protection, exorcism

MAGICAL AMPLIFIERS

- ♦ **Angel:** Gabriel
- ♦ **Chakra:** Root
- ♦ **Crystals:** Moss agate, rose quartz, zircon
- ♦ **Tarot:** The Moon
- ♦ **Sacred to:** Beltane

> **DIY TIP:** Plant mallow under the Full Moon's light, harvest the root, and use it in amulets for potency.

FOR GARDENING

Mallow is easy to grow and can be invasive.

Suggested Varieties for Beginners: Zebrina, Primley Blue

Location: USDA Plant Hardiness Zone 3–8

Light: Full sun

Water and Food: Regular watering, add compost twice during the growing season

Soil, Pot, Cultivation: Average soil, grow in 12-inch pots, cut to the ground in autumn

MANDRAKE

Mandragora officinarum

Size: 6 to 16 inches

Parts Used: Root, leaves, flowers, berries

Safety Considerations: Poisonous to humans and pets. Wear gloves when handling.

Planetary Ruler: Mercury

Moon Phase: Waning

Element: Earth

Zodiac Sign: Taurus

Gender: Masculine

Deity: Circe, Hecate, Saturn

Lore: Magic lore tells us that the mandrake root must be harvested carefully, or the root will utter enraged screams when dug up.

Magical Purpose: Fertility, protection, spirit world

MAGICAL AMPLIFIERS

- ♦ **Angel:** Uriel
- ♦ **Chakra:** Root
- ♦ **Crystals:** Black tourmaline, obsidian, pyrite
- ♦ **Tarot:** The Emperor

DIY TIP: To activate a mandrake root, place it on your altar, undisturbed, for 3 days, and soak it in warm water overnight; then the root will be ready to use for spells and rituals.

FOR GARDENING

Mandrake is a perennial plant with a stemless tuft of leaves with flowers appearing in the center of the plant.

Location: USDA Plant Hardiness Zone 6–8; usually grown as an indoor container plant

Light: Place under grow lights or put the pot outdoors in full sun

Water and Food: Regular watering, fertilize once in early spring

Soil, Pot, Cultivation: Well-drained soil, grow in 12-inch pots that are at least 12 inches deep, grow from seed

MARIGOLD

Calendula officinalis

Size: 10 to 12 inches

Parts Used: Flowers

Safety Considerations: Edible. Nontoxic for humans and pets.

Planetary Ruler: Sun

Moon Phase: Waxing

Element: Air, Fire

Zodiac Sign: Cancer, Leo

Gender: Masculine

Deity: Xochiquetzal

Lore: In Greek mythology, four wood nymphs who had been transformed into white marigolds were painted gold by Apollo's sunrays when he took pity on them.

Magical Purpose: Divination, dreams, omens, peace

MAGICAL AMPLIFIERS

- ♦ **Angel:** Michael
- ♦ **Chakra:** Solar Plexus
- ♦ **Crystals:** Aquamarine, tiger's-eye
- ♦ **Tarot:** The Hanged Man
- ♦ **Sacred to:** Beltane, Mabon

> **DIY TIP:** Make calendula oil by steeping equal amounts of dried petals with olive oil in a glass for 2 weeks.

FOR GARDENING

Cheerful marigold flowers attract pollinators, repel pests, and have healing properties. Pinch back young plants for busy growth.

Suggested Varieties for Beginners: Prince, Dwarf Gem

Location: USDA Plant Hardiness Zone 3–10

Light: Full sun

Water and Food: Regular watering, feed once in the spring

Soil, Pot, Cultivation: Average soil with good drainage, grow in any size pot, soil for pots should be a mixture of half soil and half compost

MARJORAM
Origanum majorana

Size: 1 to 2 feet

Parts Used: Leaves

Safety Considerations: Edible. Toxic to pets, nontoxic for humans.

Planetary Ruler: Mercury

Moon Phase: Full

Element: Air

Zodiac Sign: Aries

Gender: Masculine

Deity: Aphrodite, Venus

Lore: Marjoram probably originated from the Mediterranean region and has been used since ancient times. The ancient Greeks used it medicinally, and young couples were crowned with marjoram wreaths during wedding ceremonies to ensure a happy, loving married life.

Magical Purpose: Love, happiness, health, wealth

MAGICAL AMPLIFIERS

- ♦ **Angel:** Raphael
- ♦ **Chakras:** Root, Heart
- ♦ **Crystals:** Bloodstone, rose quartz, rhodochrosite, topaz
- ♦ **Tarot:** The Empress

DIY TIP: Add marjoram to food dishes to promote love and happiness, or carry some in your pocket to attract wealth.

FOR GARDENING

Marjoram is easy to care for and makes an attractive indoor herb plant.

Suggested Varieties for Beginners: Sweet marjoram

Location: USDA Plant Hardiness Zone 6–11

Light: Full sun

Water and Food: Light to regular watering, doesn't require fertilizer

Soil, Pot, Cultivation: Average soil with good drainage, grow in 6-inch pots, harvest just before the flowers open

MEADOWSWEET

Filipendula ulmaria

Size: 4 feet

Parts Used: Flowers, leaves, root

Safety Considerations: Nontoxic for humans and pets.

Planetary Ruler: Jupiter

Moon Phase: Waxing

Element: Air

Zodiac Sign: Gemini

Gender: Masculine

Deity: Blodeuwedd, Aine

Lore: Meadowsweet has been a medicinal herb since ancient times and is a natural remedy for headaches when taken as a tea. In medieval times, meadowsweet was used during festivals and worn as bridal garlands.

Magical Purpose: Love, divination, peace

MAGICAL AMPLIFIERS

- **Angel:** Chamuel
- **Chakra:** Root
- **Crystals:** Emerald, turquoise, lapis lazuli
- **Tarot:** The Empress
- **Sacred to:** Midsummer

DIY TIP: Use dried meadowsweet in dream pillows to cheer the heart and encourage peace. To entice fairies to live in your garden, plant meadowsweet.

FOR GARDENING

Meadowsweet is a perennial shrub with scented clusters of white flowers that bloom all summer.

Suggested Varieties for Beginners: Common meadowsweet

Location: USDA Plant Hardiness Zone 3–8

Light: Full sun to part shade

Water and Food: Generous watering, add compost in the spring

Soil, Pot, Cultivation: Regular moist soil, grow in 20-inch pots, divide the roots every 3 years

MINT

Mentha spp.

Size: 1 to 2 feet

Parts Used: Leaves

Safety Considerations: Edible. Toxic to pets, nontoxic for humans.

Planetary Ruler: Mercury

Moon Phase: Waning

Element: Air

Zodiac Sign: Gemini

Gender: Masculine

Deity: Hecate, Pluto, Hades, Nyx

Lore: Mentha gets its name from Mintha, the Greek nymph who tried to seduce Hades, the Lord of the Underworld.

Magical Purpose: Money, healing, travel, spirit world, protection

MAGICAL AMPLIFIERS

- ◆ **Angel:** Raphael
- ◆ **Chakra:** Root
- ◆ **Crystals:** Bloodstone, malachite, moss agate
- ◆ **Tarot:** The Magician

DIY TIP: Chew mint leaves to settle an upset stomach and sweeten the breath.

FOR GARDENING

Mint is very easy to grow and spreads through underground runners. It's invasive, so grow it in a container or confined garden bed.

Suggested Varieties for Beginners: Common mint

Location: USDA Plant Hardiness Zone 3–8

Light: Full sun to part shade

Water and Food: Regular watering, apply a balanced fertilizer once in spring

Soil, Pot, Cultivation: Will grow in any soil and any pot or container if it's well drained

MISTLETOE

Viscum album

Size: 3 inches to 5 feet

Parts Used: Whole plant

Safety Considerations: Toxic for humans and pets. All parts of mistletoe are toxic if ingested; always wear gloves when handling.

Planetary Ruler: Sun

Moon Phase: Waning

Element: Air

Zodiac Sign: Leo

Gender: Masculine

Deity: Apollo, Frigga, Odin

Lore: Druid priests cut mistletoe for ceremonial use after receiving a vision telling them to do so. The custom of gathering, decorating homes with, and kissing under the mistletoe at Christmas is a survival of Druid magic.

Magical Purpose: Dreamwork, exorcism, fertility, love

MAGICAL AMPLIFIERS
- **Angel:** Jophiel
- **Chakra:** Crown
- **Crystals:** Amethyst, sapphire, sugilite
- **Tarot:** Wheel of Fortune
- **Sacred to:** Litha, Yule

DIY TIP: Squash mature berries into the lower side of a tree branch in late fall to propagate mistletoe. Wait until spring to see if the plant begins to grow.

FOR GARDENING

Mistletoe is a parasitic plant that attaches itself to a host tree or shrub to gain nutrients and water.

Suggested Varieties for Beginners: American mistletoe

Location: USDA Plant Hardiness Zone 5–9

Light: Part shade to full shade

Water and Food: Keep soil moist

Soil, Pot, Cultivation: Mistletoe prefers to grow on hardwood trees such as oak, ash, or elm. Seeds can be started in soil but must be placed on a host tree once sprouted.

THE GREEN WITCH'S HERB AND PLANT ENCYCLOPEDIA

MORINGA

Moringa oleifera

Size: 25 to 35 feet

Parts Used: Leaves, flowers, pods, root

Safety Considerations: Edible. Nontoxic for humans and pets.

Planetary Ruler: Sun

Moon Phase: Waxing

Element: Fire

Zodiac Sign: Leo

Gender: Masculine

Lore: Moringa is touted as one of nature's most nutritious plants, and its leaves have been found in ancient Egyptian tombs.

Magical Purpose: Health, courage, strength

MAGICAL AMPLIFIERS

♦ **Angel:** Michael
♦ **Chakra:** Throat
♦ **Crystals:** Amber, citrine, topaz
♦ **Tarot:** The Sun

DIY TIP: Harvest the older leaves and pods when they are ½ inch in diameter. The edible pods are ready when they easily pop off the branches.

FOR GARDENING

Moringa is a fast-growing tree called the "miracle tree" because of its beneficial nutritional and medicinal qualities.

Location: USDA Plant Hardiness Zone 10–11, grow as a houseplant in cooler climates

Light: Full sun

Water and Food: Regular water, but water daily until 18 inches tall; add compost when planting

Soil, Pot, Cultivation: Average soil, grow in 30-inch pots, regularly prune to encourage bushy growth

MOSS

Bryophyta

Size: 1 to 2 inches

Parts Used: Whole plant

Safety Considerations: Nontoxic for humans and pets.

Planetary Ruler: Moon

Moon Phase: Full

Element: Water

Zodiac Sign: Pisces, Cancer

Gender: Feminine

Deity: Aphrodite, Luna, Selene

Lore: Moss people from German folklore are a race of elves with hair and clothing made entirely of moss.

Magical Purpose: Luck, prosperity

MAGICAL AMPLIFIERS

- **Angel:** Ariel
- **Chakra:** Solar Plexus
- **Crystals:** Amazonite, amethyst, labradorite
- **Tarot:** The Wheel of Fortune

FOR FORAGING

Moss grows very slowly, so when foraging, leave half of the moss clump so it can recover. Forage throughout North America. USDA Plant Hardiness Zone 9–11

DIY TIP: Moss is easy to transplant; keep it watered. Use dried moss to stuff poppets.

MUGWORT
Artemisia vulgaris

Size: 6 feet

Parts Used: Leaves, flowers

Safety Considerations: Edible. For humans, nontoxic in small amounts; for pets, toxic.

Planetary Ruler: Venus

Moon Phase: Full

Element: Earth, Air

Zodiac Sign: Cancer, Gemini, Libra, Sagittarius

Gender: Feminine

Deity: Artemis, Diana

Lore: Mugwort was traditionally gathered on Saint John's Eve and worn as a crown to protect from possession, disease, and bad luck.

Magical Purpose: Banishing, divination, messages, spirits

MAGICAL AMPLIFIERS

- **Angel:** Gabriel
- **Chakra:** Third Eye
- **Crystals:** Ruby, sapphire
- **Tarot:** The Emperor
- **Sacred to:** Samhain

DIY TIP: Use mugwort to season fish and meat; it's a traditional seasoning for Christmas goose in Germany.

FOR GARDENING

Mugwort grows just about anywhere and will be more aromatic if grown in dry conditions.

Suggested Varieties for Beginners: Common mugwort

Location: USDA Plant Hardiness Zone 4–8

Light: Full sun

Water and Food: Regular watering, add compost and balanced fertilizer once a year

Soil, Pot, Cultivation: Moist, well-drained soil; can be invasive; plant in 12-inch pots; the roots spread underground and will need to be controlled

MULLEIN

Verbascum thapus

Size: 2 to 7 feet

Parts Used: Flowers, leaves

Safety Considerations: Edible. Nontoxic for humans and pets.

Planetary Ruler: Saturn

Moon Phase: Waning

Element: Fire

Zodiac Sign: Leo

Gender: Feminine

Deity: Jupiter

Lore: Roman ladies soaked mullein flowers in water and used the liquid to dye their hair yellow.

Magical Purpose: Courage, protection, health, divination, exorcism

MAGICAL AMPLIFIERS

- **Angel:** Michael
- **Chakra:** Heart
- **Crystals:** Sunstone, carnelian, tiger's-eye
- **Tarot:** Strength

FOR FORAGING

The dried leaves and flowers make a healing tea, and an oil infusion made with the flowers is good for ear infections. Forage throughout North America. USDA Plant Hardiness Zone 3–9

DIY TIP: To know if your lover is faithful, bend a mullein plant toward the lover's house. If the plant resumes its upright position, your lover is devoted.

MUSTARD

Brassica spp.

Size: 12 to 18 inches

Parts Used: Seeds, leaves

Safety Considerations: Edible. Toxic to pets, nontoxic for humans.

Planetary Ruler: Mars

Moon Phase: Full

Element: Fire

Zodiac Sign: Aries

Gender: Masculine

Deity: Aesculapius

Lore: It's believed that mustard was first cultivated in India around 3000 BCE. The Romans created the first mustard condiment by mixing the crushed seeds with grape juice.

Magical Purpose: Control, justice, power, success

MAGICAL AMPLIFIERS

♦ **Angel:** Chamuel
♦ **Chakra:** Sacral
♦ **Crystals:** Citrine, smoky quartz, sunstone
♦ **Tarot:** The Emperor

DIY TIP: To harvest the seeds, allow the plants to mature and harvest the pods when the plants begin to yellow but before the pods break open.

FOR GARDENING

Mustards are cool-season plants that grow quickly and then bolt. Sow every 3 weeks for a continual harvest.

Suggested Varieties for Beginners: Red Giant

Location: USDA Plant Hardiness Zone 4-9

Light: Full sun to part shade

Water and Food: Regular watering, add compost and balanced fertilizer when planting

Soil, Pot, Cultivation: Average soil, grow in pots that are 6 inches deep, keep the soil moist

NASTURTIUM

Tropaeolum majus

Size: 6 to 12 inches

Parts Used: Flowers, seeds

Safety Considerations: Edible. Nontoxic for humans and pets.

Planetary Ruler: Neptune

Moon Phase: Waning

Element: Air

Zodiac Sign: Libra

Gender: Feminine

Deity: Belenos, Sulis

Lore: *Nasturtium* comes from the Latin word *nasus tortus* meaning "convulsed nose," referring to people's faces when tasting the spicy plant.

Magical Purpose: Banishing, creativity, freedom, protection, strength, purity

MAGICAL AMPLIFIERS

- **Angel:** Gabriel
- **Chakra:** Solar Plexus
- **Crystals:** Bloodstone, citrine, sunstone, topaz
- **Tarot:** The Hanged Man

> **DIY TIP:** Grow as a companion plant with pumpkins, melons, cucumbers, and broccoli to protect them from pests.

FOR GARDENING

Nasturtiums add a splash of color to every garden and are very easy to grow. They thrive in poor soil and don't need extra fertilization.

Suggested Varieties for Beginners: Alaska, Apricot, Peach Melba

Location: USDA Plant Hardiness Zone 9–11

Light: Full sun to part shade, protect from the harsh afternoon sun

Water and Food: Regular watering, no fertilizer

Soil, Pot, Cultivation: Average soil, grow in 12-inch pots, cut back once in the summer to promote bloom

NETTLE

Urtica dioica

Size: 3 to 7 feet

Parts Used: Leaves, stems

Safety Considerations: Edible. Nontoxic for humans and pets.

Planetary Ruler: Mars

Moon Phase: Waning

Element: Fire

Zodiac Sign: Leo

Gender: Masculine

Deity: Loki, Thor

Lore: Nettles were used as protection against "elf-shot," a mysterious illness caused by being struck by an elf's arrow.

Magical Purpose: Exorcism, protection, healing

MAGICAL AMPLIFIERS

♦ **Angel:** Raphael
♦ **Chakra:** Root
♦ **Crystals:** Black tourmaline, clear quartz
♦ **Tarot:** The Star

FOR FORAGING

Stinging nettle can be invasive. Forage throughout North America. USDA Plant Hardiness Zone 4–10

DIY TIP: To harvest nettles, cut back the top third of the plant and wear gloves. Cook nettle before eating to remove the sting.

OXEYE DAISY
Leucanthemum vulgare

Size: 26 inches

Parts Used: Flowers, leaves

Safety Considerations: Edible. For humans, nontoxic in small amounts; for pets, toxic.

Planetary Ruler: Venus

Moon Phase: Full

Element: Water

Zodiac Sign: Scorpio

Gender: Feminine

Deity: Freya, Thor

Lore: The Scots called daisies "gools" when they invaded their pastures and fields. If they had too many gools, they had to pay a special tax.

Magical Purpose: Lust, love

FOR FORAGING

Oxeye daisy petals and leaves are edible in small amounts. Daisy petal tea can be used for coughs, colds, and fevers. Forage throughout North America. USDA Plant Hardiness Zone 1–8

MAGICAL AMPLIFIERS

- ◆ **Angel:** Chamuel
- ◆ **Chakra:** Heart
- ◆ **Crystals:** Red jasper, serpentine, carnelian
- ◆ **Tarot:** Strength

> **DIY TIP:** Pluck the petals from a daisy to discover if they "love you" or "love you not."

THE GREEN WITCH'S HERB AND PLANT ENCYCLOPEDIA

PANSY
Viola tricolor

Size: 6 inches

Parts Used: Flowers, leaves, seeds

Safety Considerations: Edible. Nontoxic for humans and pets.

Planetary Ruler: Saturn

Moon Phase: New

Element: Water

Zodiac Sign: Scorpio

Gender: Feminine

Deity: Aphrodite, Zeus

Lore: Legend has it that the original pansies were pure white until they were pierced by Cupid's arrow and transformed into the colorful flowers we know today.

Magical Purpose: Rain magic, love, divination

MAGICAL AMPLIFIERS

- ◆ **Angel:** Jophiel
- ◆ **Chakra:** Heart
- ◆ **Crystals:** Jade, topaz
- ◆ **Tarot:** The High Priest

DIY TIP: Make pansy ice cubes by filling the tray half full of water and adding a pansy to each tray. Freeze until solid; then top up with water and freeze again.

FOR GARDENING

Pansies bloom from spring to fall and prefer cool weather. They spread profusely through self-seeding.

Suggested Varieties for Beginners: Heart's delight, heartsease

Location: USDA Plant Hardiness Zone 8–11

Light: Full sun to part shade

Water and Food: Regular watering, fertilize monthly with a balanced fertilizer

Soil, Pot, Cultivation: Loamy, sandy soil, self-seeds, grow in 12-inch pots, cut back after flowering to encourage new blooms

PARSLEY

Petroselinum crispum

Size: 9 to 12 inches

Parts Used: Leaves

Safety Considerations: Edible. Toxic to pets, nontoxic for humans.

Planetary Ruler: Mercury

Moon Phase: New

Element: Air

Zodiac Sign: Gemini

Gender: Masculine

Deity: Persephone

Lore: Parsley has a long germination time and a very long taproot, so legend has it that the parsley seeds had to journey to the Underworld and back before they could grow. Persephone is often shown holding a sprig of parsley.

Magical Purpose: Death, lust, protection, purification

MAGICAL AMPLIFIERS

◆ **Angel:** Raphael
◆ **Chakra:** Root
◆ **Crystals:** Agate, citrine, quartz, tiger's-eye
◆ **Tarot:** The Magician

> **DIY TIP:** Snip off ground-level leaves as needed; pruning encourages new growth.

FOR GARDENING

Parsley is easy to grow and has few pest or disease issues.

Suggested Varieties for Beginners: Common parsley

Location: USDA Plant Hardiness Zone 3–11

Light: Full sun to part sun

Water and Food: Regular watering, fertilize twice during the growing season

Soil, Pot, Cultivation: Well-drained soil with added compost; grows in 14-inch pots; start seed outdoors in late spring, indoors 6 to 8 weeks before the last frost date

PASSIONFLOWER

Passiflora incarnata

Size: 10 to 20 feet

Parts Used: Leaves, flowers, stems, fruit

Safety Considerations: Toxic to pets, nontoxic for humans. *Passiflora incarnata* is nontoxic to humans if ingested in small amounts, but other varieties of passionflower are toxic.

Planetary Ruler: Venus

Moon Phase: Waning

Element: Water

Zodiac Sign: Libra

Gender: Feminine

Deity: Jesus

Lore: Passionflower was used as a sedative by the Cherokee and Choctaw tribes. It was brought to Europe by the Spanish.

Magical Purpose: Money, lust, sleep

MAGICAL AMPLIFIERS

♦ **Angel:** Zadkiel
♦ **Chakra:** Third Eye
♦ **Crystals:** Amethyst, rose quartz, selenite
♦ **Tarot:** The Universe

> **DIY TIP:** Passionflower is very difficult to grow from seeds, and seed-grown plants may take more than 10 years to flower.

FOR GARDENING

Purple passionflower or "maypop" is a fast-growing, climbing evergreen vine with striking, scented flowers.

Suggested Varieties for Beginners: Purple passionflower

Location: USDA Plant Hardiness Zone 7–11

Light: Full sun to part shade

Water and Food: Regular watering, apply mulch, low-nitrogen fertilizer monthly during the growing season

Soil, Pot, Cultivation: Average soil; use a pot 3 inches larger than the root ball; fruit is ripe when it turns green, doesn't require pruning

PENNYROYAL

Mentha pulegium

Size: 6 to 12 inches

Parts Used: Leaves, stems, flowers

Safety Considerations: Toxic for humans and pets. All parts of pennyroyal are toxic if ingested; always wear gloves when handling. If you're pregnant, be extra careful when handling this plant.

Planetary Ruler: Mars

Moon Phase: Waxing

Element: Fire

Zodiac Sign: Libra

Gender: Masculine

Deity: Demeter

Lore: The ancient Romans used pennyroyal to repel fleas and insects.

Magical Purpose: Strength, protection, peace

MAGICAL AMPLIFIERS

- **Angel:** Michael
- **Chakras:** Root, Solar Plexus
- **Crystals:** Amber, carnelian, tiger's-eye
- **Tarot:** The Sun

> **DIY TIP:** Pennyroyal makes an excellent ground cover in poor soil and is a beautiful addition to hanging baskets.

FOR GARDENING

Pennyroyal is a member of the mint family and is a fast-growing plant with small purple blooms.

Suggested Varieties for Beginners: European pennyroyal

Location: USDA Plant Hardiness Zone 6–9

Light: Full sun to part shade

Water and Food: Regular watering, fertilizer is not required

Soil, Pot, Cultivation: Rich, moist soil; grow in 12-inch pots; spreads aggressively, so cut it back regularly

PEONY
Paeonia

Size: 3 feet

Parts Used: Flowers, seeds, root

Safety Considerations: Toxic for humans and pets. All parts of the peony are toxic if ingested in large amounts. Plants are safe to handle without gloves.

Planetary Ruler: Sun

Moon Phase: Waning

Element: Fire

Zodiac Sign: Leo

Gender: Masculine

Deity: Pan

Lore: The underworld god Pluto was wounded by an arrow and healed by Paeon, a medical student of the god of Healing, Asklepios. In a jealous rage, Asklepios murdered Paeon, who was brought back to life as a peony flower by the god Zeus.

Magical Purpose: Protection, exorcism

MAGICAL AMPLIFIERS

♦ **Angel:** Uriel
♦ **Chakra:** Solar Plexus
♦ **Crystals:** Agate, howlite, smoky quartz
♦ **Tarot:** The Tower

FOR GARDENING

Peony is a large spring-flowering perennial with huge, fragrant blooms.

Suggested Varieties for Beginners: Big Ben, Pillow Talk

Location: USDA Plant Hardiness Zone 3–9

Light: Full sun

Water and Food: Generous watering, add compost in the spring

Soil, Pot, Cultivation: Well-drained, fertile, slightly acidic soil; grow in 18-inch-deep and wide pots; pruning is not required

DIY TIP: Peonies make excellent cut flowers. Pick them when they are still in bud, remove all the lower leaves, and put the stems in a vase of lukewarm water.

PEPPERMINT

Mentha piperita

Size: 1 to 2 feet

Parts Used: Leaves

Safety Considerations: Edible. Toxic to pets, nontoxic for humans.

Planetary Ruler: Mercury

Moon Phase: Waning

Element: Fire, Air

Zodiac Sign: Aquarius, Aries, Gemini, Virgo

Gender: Masculine

Deity: Pluto, Zeus

Lore: The Egyptians were the first to cultivate peppermint, and a thirteenth-century Icelandic medical text mentioned peppermint.

Magical Purpose: Purification, awareness, dream spells, visions

MAGICAL AMPLIFIERS

- ◆ **Angel:** Raphael
- ◆ **Chakra:** Crown
- ◆ **Crystals:** Bloodstone, peridot, sapphire, tourmaline
- ◆ **Tarot:** The Hermit

DIY TIP: Use the leaves to relieve bee stings, burns, and toothaches. Drink peppermint tea to relieve an upset stomach. Peppermint leaves repel flies and mice.

FOR GARDENING

Propagate peppermint through root division and cuttings. Peppermint is invasive, so contain the roots.

Suggested Varieties for Beginners: Common peppermint

Location: USDA Plant Hardiness Zone 5–10

Light: Full sun to part shade

Water and Food: Regular watering, apply a balanced fertilizer once in spring

Soil, Pot, Cultivation: Grows in any soil, pot, or container if it's well drained

PERIWINKLE

Vinca minor

Size: 3 to 6 inches

Parts Used: Flowers, leaves

Safety Considerations: Toxic for humans and pets. All parts of the periwinkle are toxic, but the plants are safe to handle.

Planetary Ruler: Mercury, Venus

Moon Phase: Full

Element: Water

Zodiac Sign: Scorpio

Gender: Feminine

Deity: Aphrodite

Lore: In the wedding poem "something old, something new, something borrowed, something blue," periwinkle was traditionally the "something blue." Periwinkle vine wrapped around the bride's thigh promoted fertility.

Magical Purpose: Binding spells, marriage, love

MAGICAL AMPLIFIERS

- ◆ **Angel:** Chamuel
- ◆ **Chakra:** Heart
- ◆ **Crystals:** Amethyst, agate, rose quartz
- ◆ **Tarot:** The Lovers

FOR FORAGING

Be sure to wash your hands after touching periwinkle. Forage in urban areas and private land with permission. USDA Plant Hardiness Zone 4–9

DIY TIP: Periwinkle is easy to weave into floral crowns worn during handfasting or marriage rites.

PINE

Pinus

Size: 3 to 200 feet

Parts Used: Needles, branches, bark, nuts

Safety Considerations: Edible. Mildly toxic for humans and pets.

Planetary Ruler: Mars

Moon Phase: Waxing

Element: Air

Zodiac Sign: Aries

Gender: Masculine

Deity: Pan, Dionysus, Venus, Astarte

Lore: When Saint Boniface, an English missionary, discovered pagans worshipping a sacred oak tree, he cut it down and decreed the pine (or evergreen) as the new holy tree of Christianity.

Magical Purpose: Healing, fertility, protection, exorcism

MAGICAL AMPLIFIERS

- **Angel:** Raphael
- **Chakra:** Root
- **Crystals:** Citrine, turquoise, tiger's-eye
- **Tarot:** The Magician

FOR FORAGING

Pine nuts and pollen are entirely edible, and pine needles are fine to consume in small quantities and can soothe sore throats and fight infection. Pine needle tea is healing and high in vitamin C. Forage throughout North America. USDA Plant Hardiness Zone 4–8

DIY TIP: Stuff pine cones with lard and roll them in birdseed as a winter treat for wild birds.

PLANTAIN
Plantago major

Size: 3 to 4 inches

Parts Used: Flowers, leaves, root

Safety Considerations: Edible. Nontoxic for humans and pets.

Planetary Ruler: Venus

Moon Phase: Waxing

Element: Earth

Zodiac Sign: Taurus

Gender: Feminine

Deity: Demeter

Lore: Puritans are thought to have brought plantain to North America from Europe.

Magical Purpose: Healing, strength, protection

MAGICAL AMPLIFIERS
- **Angel:** Michael
- **Chakra:** Solar Plexus
- **Crystals:** Agate, citrine, smoky quartz
- **Tarot:** Strength

DIY TIP: Use young, fresh leaves in salads and cook older leaves in soups and stews. Leaves can be made into a poultice for wounds or used to soothe insect bites, sunburn, and poison ivy. Plantain tea will help with stomach issues.

FOR FORAGING

Plantain is a persistent, common weed that has naturalized across North America. Forage throughout North America. USDA Plant Hardiness Zone 3–12

POISON HEMLOCK

Conium maculatum

Size: 5 to 10 feet

Parts Used: Leaves and berries

Safety Considerations: Poisonous to humans and pets. All parts are deadly poison if ingested; the plant will also burn your skin if touched; if you must handle it, wear gloves and long sleeves.

Planetary Ruler: Saturn

Moon Phase: Dark

Element: Water

Zodiac Sign: Scorpio

Gender: Feminine

Deity: Hecate

Lore: Poison hemlock is traditionally associated with European witchcraft and was said to be one of the essential plants grown in the witch's garden. It was planted at the front and back of the house to stop baneful energy from entering.

Magical Purpose: Astral projection, baneful magic

MAGICAL AMPLIFIERS

- ◆ **Angel:** Azrael
- ◆ **Chakra:** Crown
- ◆ **Crystals:** Amethyst, aquamarine, Apache tear
- ◆ **Tarot:** Death

FOR FORAGING

Poison hemlock grows throughout North America in disturbed areas, roadsides, and trails and alongside streams. This plant should never be cultivated in the home garden and has been included in this book simply because it's a traditional witch-craft plant.

DIY TIP: Poison hemlock can be identified by its highly unpleasant smell when bruised.

POPLAR

Populus

Size: 20 to 50 feet

Parts Used: Leaves, twigs, bark, buds

Safety Considerations: Edible. Nontoxic for humans and pets.

Planetary Ruler: Saturn

Moon Phase: Full

Element: Water

Zodiac Sign: Pisces

Gender: Feminine

Deity: Hades

Lore: Poplar is one of the ingredients mentioned in Witch's Flying Oil, a secret oil that helped witches "fly"! It didn't help with literal flying—it was a mixture of ingredients that was rubbed onto the skin to induce visions.

Magical Purpose: Money, flying

MAGICAL AMPLIFIERS

- Angel: Gabriel
- Chakra: Root
- Crystals: Moonstone, labradorite, rhodonite
- Tarot: The Fool

FOR FORAGING

An infused oil made with poplar buds can help with inflammation and pain. Poplar bud tea reduces fever, coughs, and cold symptoms. Forage throughout North America. USDA Plant Hardiness Zone 1–6

DIY TIP: Prepare Balm of Gilead by covering the buds in olive oil and warming the mixture in a slow cooker for 2 or 3 hours.

POPPY

Papaver

Size: 28 inches

Parts Used: Flowers, leaves, seeds

Safety Considerations: Toxic to pets, nontoxic for humans.

Planetary Ruler: Moon

Moon Phase: Waning

Element: Water

Zodiac Sign: Capricorn

Gender: Feminine

Deity: Hecate, Hypnos, Lilith, Morpheus

Lore: The seeds of poppies can remain dormant for more than 50 years and then germinate once their soil is disturbed.

Magical Purpose: Astral travel, sleep, spirit world, visions

MAGICAL AMPLIFIERS

- **Angel:** Uriel
- **Chakra:** Solar Plexus
- **Crystals:** Clear quartz, lapis lazuli, obsidian
- **Tarot:** The Moon

> **DIY TIP:** Poppy seeds are a safe alternative to use in place of poisonous herbs like belladonna and aconite.

FOR GARDENING

Poppy is an annual wildflower that blooms from late spring to early summer. Poppies are low maintenance and work well in cottage and pollinator gardens.

Suggested Varieties for Beginners: Shirley poppy

Location: USDA Plant Hardiness Zone 1–10

Light: Full sun to part shade

Water and Food: Light watering, fertilizer is not required

Soil, Pot, Cultivation: Average to poor, well-drained soil; grow in 12-inch pots; deadhead spent flowers

PURSLANE

Portulaca oleracea

Size: 3 inches

Parts Used: Leaves, stems, flowers, seeds

Safety Considerations: Edible. Toxic to pets, nontoxic for humans.

Planetary Ruler: Moon

Moon Phase: Full

Element: Water

Zodiac Sign: Cancer

Gender: Feminine

Deity: Luna

Lore: Pliny the Elder, a Roman philosopher who lived around 50 CE, recommended that people carry amulets containing purslane to prevent sickness.

Magical Purpose: Sleep, love, luck

MAGICAL AMPLIFIERS

♦ **Angel:** Raphael
♦ **Chakra:** Third Eye
♦ **Crystals:** Black tourmaline, chrysoprase, moldavite
♦ **Tarot:** The Moon

FOR FORAGING

The leaves, stems, and flower buds are edible and taste tart and salty. Forage throughout North America. USDA Plant Hardiness Zone 5-10

DIY TIP: Purslane is a nutritious addition when used raw in salads or cooked in soups and stews. It is a potent plant source of omega-3 acids typically found in fish oil.

QUEEN ANNE'S LACE

Daucus carota

Size: 8 to 45 inches

Parts Used: Flowers

Safety Considerations: Edible with certain identification, though can cause issues with fertility. Nontoxic for humans and pets.

Planetary Ruler: Mercury

Moon Phase: Waxing

Element: Air

Zodiac Sign: Gemini

Gender: Feminine

Deity: Aphrodite, Hermes, Venus

Lore: Queen Anne's lace arrived in North America in the seventeenth century and naturalized throughout the continent. The name is said to have come from its resemblance to the headdress of Queen Anne of Denmark.

Magical Purpose: Fertility, beauty

MAGICAL AMPLIFIERS

- ♦ **Angel:** Jophiel
- ♦ **Chakra:** Crown
- ♦ **Crystals:** Amethyst, sodalite, red jasper
- ♦ **Tarot:** The Empress

FOR GARDENING

The flowers are edible and can be added to salads. Add the seeds to flavor soups and stews. Forage throughout North America. USDA Plant Hardiness Zone 3-10

DIY TIP: The single red flower in the center can be a substitution for blood in spells, rituals, and potions.

RASPBERRY

Rubus idaeus

Size: 4 to 6 feet

Parts Used: Leaves, fruit

Safety Considerations: Edible. Toxic to pets with exception of the berries; nontoxic for humans, but those who are pregnant or breastfeeding should not ingest raspberry leaves.

Planetary Ruler: Moon, Venus

Moon Phase: Full

Element: Water

Zodiac Sign: Cancer, Pisces

Gender: Feminine

Deity: Hera

Lore: According to Greek legend, raspberries got their red color when Zeus's nursemaid pricked her finger while picking the snow-white berries.

Magical Purpose: Fertility, love, protection

MAGICAL AMPLIFIERS

♦ **Angel:** Gabriel
♦ **Chakra:** Root
♦ **Crystals:** Amber, bloodstone
♦ **Tarot:** The Empress

DIY TIP: Raspberries make a delicious cordial when fermented with orange juice and sugar.

FOR GARDENING

There are two types of raspberries: summer bearing and everbearing. Summer-bearing canes produce a single crop of berries; everbearing canes produce two crops.

Suggested Varieties for Beginners: Latham (summer bearing), Caroline (everbearing)

Location: USDA Plant Hardiness Zone 4–8

Light: Full sun to part shade

Water and Food: Regular watering, use high-nitrogen fertilizer or manure once a year

Soil, Pot, Cultivation: Rich, well-drained soil high in organics; grow in 24-inch to 36-inch pots; cut canes down to the ground in the fall

RHODODENDRON

Rhododendron

Size: 12 to 25 feet

Parts Used: Flowers

Safety Considerations: Toxic for humans and pets. All parts of rhododendron are mildly toxic if ingested but can be safely handled without gloves.

Planetary Ruler: Venus

Moon Phase: Full

Element: Water

Zodiac Sign: Cancer

Gender: Female

Deity: Andromeda

Lore: In the language of flowers, *rhododendron* means "everything will be better because of you."

Magical Purpose: Personal power, protection, mystery

MAGICAL AMPLIFIERS

- **Angel:** Chamuel
- **Chakra:** Solar Plexus
- **Crystals:** Carnelian, citrine, rose quartz
- **Tarot:** Strength

> **DIY TIP:** If your rhododendron is in a sunny location, it will be compact and shrub-like; if it's in a shadier spot, it will become more like a tree.

FOR GARDENING

Rhododendrons are large evergreen shrubs that flower profusely in the spring and early summer.

Suggested Varieties for Beginners: Pacific rhododendron

Location: USDA Plant Hardiness Zone 4–8

Light: Full sun to part shade

Water and Food: Generous watering, give a small amount of acid-loving plant fertilizer while blooming

Soil, Pot, Cultivation: Acidic soil with low nutrients, grow in pots 3 inches larger than the root ball, remove dead flowers and prune to keep compact

ROSE

Rosa spp.

Size: 4 to 6 feet

Parts Used: Flowers, fruit, leaves

Safety Considerations: Edible. Nontoxic for humans and pets.

Planetary Ruler: Venus

Moon Phase: Waxing

Element: Water

Zodiac Sign: Leo, Taurus

Gender: Feminine

Deity: Venus

Lore: Roses were first cultivated in China. Anacreon, the Greek poet, said that when Aphrodite emerged from the sea, the foam that dripped from her body turned into white roses.

Magical Purpose: Clarity, love, childbirth, trust

MAGICAL AMPLIFIERS

- ◆ **Angel:** Gabriel
- ◆ **Chakra:** Root
- ◆ **Crystals:** Carnelian, cat's-eye
- ◆ **Tarot:** Justice

> **DIY TIP:** Cut roses when the buds are just beginning to open and recut the stems before putting them in a vase.

FOR GARDENING

Rosa species are easy-care plants that can handle less-than-perfect growing conditions. Remove unwanted suckers around the base and prune as needed to maintain a neat shape.

Suggested Varieties for Beginners: Grandiflora, Bonica

Location: USDA Plant Hardiness Zone 7–10

Light: Full sun

Water and Food: Regular watering, fertilize monthly

Soil, Pot, Cultivation: Add compost and manure to the soil, grow in at least 12-inch pots, prune in early spring

ROSEMARY

Rosmarinus officinalis

Size: 4 feet

Parts Used: Leaves, branches

Safety Considerations: Edible. Toxic to pets, nontoxic for humans.

Planetary Ruler: Sun

Moon Phase: Waning

Element: Fire

Zodiac Sign: Aquarius, Aries, Leo, Sagittarius, Virgo

Gender: Masculine

Deity: Aphrodite

Lore: Rosemary was a sacred embalming herb used by the Egyptians in mummification rituals.

Magical Purpose: Memory, protection, reversal, sorrow, spirits, wisdom

MAGICAL AMPLIFIERS

- ♦ **Angel:** Michael
- ♦ **Chakra:** Third Eye
- ♦ **Crystals:** Apache tears, obsidian
- ♦ **Tarot:** Strength
- ♦ **Sacred to:** Yule

DIY TIP: Rosemary branches are easy to make into wreaths that retain their fragrance and color. Place sprigs of rosemary in drawers to protect clothing from moths.

FOR GARDENING

Rosemary is virtually disease- and pest-free and is drought tolerant once established. Prune after blooming.

Suggested Varieties for Beginners: Arp, Blue Spires

Location: USDA Plant Hardiness Zone 6–10

Light: Full sun to part sun

Water and Food: Light watering, fertilize sparingly once a year

Soil, Pot, Cultivation: Sandy, well-drained soil; grow in 12-inch pots; in cooler climates, grow in a container, and winter indoors

ROWAN

Sorbus

Size: 6 to 30 feet

Parts Used: Bark, leaves, flowers, berries

Safety Considerations: Nontoxic for humans and pets.

Planetary Ruler: Sun

Moon Phase: Waxing

Element: Fire

Zodiac Sign: Sagittarius

Gender: Masculine

Deity: Thor

Lore: In Norse mythology, a rowan tree saved the life of Thor by extending its branches over a river to keep him from drowning.

Magical Purpose: Psychic powers, healing, success

MAGICAL AMPLIFIERS

- ♦ **Angel:** Uriel
- ♦ **Chakra:** Solar Plexus
- ♦ **Crystals:** Rose quartz, selenite, tourmaline
- ♦ **Tarot:** The Magician
- ♦ **Sacred to:** Imbolc

DIY TIP: Bind rowan twigs with red thread to form a cross and hang it over doors to protect your home from negative energy.

FOR GARDENING

Rowan or mountain ash is a small deciduous tree with clusters of white or pink flowers followed by white, yellow, pink, or red berries.

Suggested Varieties for Beginners: American mountain ash

Location: USDA Plant Hardiness Zone 3–9

Light: Full sun to part shade

Water and Food: Regular watering, fertilize once in spring

Soil, Pot, Cultivation: Regular well-drained soil, not suitable for containers, does not require pruning

RUE

Ruta graveolens

Size: 2 to 3 feet

Parts Used: Leaves, stems, flowers

Safety Considerations: Toxic for humans and pets. Toxic if ingested; handling the plant may cause skin irritation, so wearing gloves is recommended.

Planetary Ruler: Mars

Moon Phase: Waning

Element: Fire

Zodiac Sign: Taurus

Gender: Masculine

Deity: Aradia, Diana

Lore: Rue has long been considered an herb of protection. It's used by the Catholic church to sprinkle holy water and mixed into incense used for exorcisms.

Magical Purpose: Hex-breaking, protection, psychic powers

MAGICAL AMPLIFIERS

- **Angel:** Michael
- **Chakra:** Throat
- **Crystals:** Amber, carnelian, topaz
- **Tarot:** The Sun

DIY TIP: Sachets made with dried rue flowers and leaves can be used to deter pests like fleas and ants.

FOR GARDENING

Rue is a short-lived perennial herb with fernlike leaves and clusters of small yellow flowers that attract butterflies.

Suggested Varieties for Beginners: Common rue

Location: USDA Plant Hardiness Zone 4–10

Light: Full sun

Water and Food: Light watering, drought tolerant, fertilizer not required

Soil, Pot, Cultivation: Regular well-drained soil; grow in 16-inch clay pots; avoid overwatering, cut the stems down to 6 inches in the spring

SAFFRON
Crocus sativus

Size: 8 to 12 inches

Parts Used: Flower stigmas

Safety Considerations: Edible. Toxic to pets, nontoxic for humans.

Planetary Ruler: Sun

Moon Phase: Waxing

Element: Fire

Zodiac Sign: Leo, Scorpio

Gender: Masculine

Deity: Eos, Ashtoreth

Lore: Saffron was a luxury item for the nobility, who offered it to their gods.

Magical Purpose: Desire, marriage, strength, happiness

MAGICAL AMPLIFIERS
- **Angel:** Michael
- **Chakras:** Root, Sacral
- **Crystals:** Diamond, sunstone, tiger's-eye
- **Tarot:** The Sun
- **Sacred to:** Litha

DIY TIP: Harvest by plucking the stigmas using a pair of tweezers. Dry the stigmas on a paper towel and keep them in an airtight container.

FOR GARDENING

The flowers are easy to grow and will multiply in your garden. The three vivid-red stigmas found in each flower are saffron.

Suggested Varieties for Beginners: *Crocus sativus*

Location: USDA Plant Hardiness Zone 6–8

Light: Full sun

Water and Food: Light watering, dryish soil, feed once a year

Soil, Pot, Cultivation: Well-drained soil with mulch and organic matter; grow in 12-inch pots; leaves grow in spring, flowers grow in fall

SAGE

Salvia officinalis

Size: 1 to 3 feet

Parts Used: Leaves

Safety Considerations: Edible. Nontoxic for humans and pets.

Planetary Ruler: Jupiter

Moon Phase: New

Element: Air, Earth

Zodiac Sign: Aquarius, Pisces, Sagittarius, Taurus

Gender: Masculine

Deity: Zeus

Lore: The first records of sage's use occurred in ancient Egypt as an herb to bring about conception.

Magical Purpose: Blessing, consecration, divination, purification, protection

MAGICAL AMPLIFIERS

♦ **Angel:** Ariel
♦ **Chakra:** Third Eye
♦ **Crystal:** Black tourmaline
♦ **Tarot:** Wheel of Fortune
♦ **Sacred to:** Mabon, Samhain, Yule

DIY TIP: Store dried sage with potatoes to help them keep longer. For better taste, freeze sage instead of drying it.

FOR GARDENING

Sage is drought tolerant and deer resistant. Cut back in spring to promote new growth.

Suggested Varieties for Beginners: Berggarten

Location: USDA Plant Hardiness Zone 4–8

Light: Full sun

Water and Food: Regular watering, drought tolerant when established; add compost in the spring, replace the entire plant when it is no longer productive

Soil, Pot, Cultivation: Average soil, soggy roots will kill the plant; grow in 12-inch pots; prune the woody stems in spring

SKULLCAP

Scutellaria lateriflora

Size: 1 to 3 feet

Parts Used: Leaves, flowers

Safety Considerations: Edible. Nontoxic for humans and pets.

Planetary Ruler: Saturn

Moon Phase: Waning

Element: Water

Zodiac Sign: Aquarius

Gender: Feminine

Deity: Hera

Lore: Skullcap is one of North America's most widely used botanicals to treat anxiety and nervousness.

Magical Purpose: Love, fidelity, peace

MAGICAL AMPLIFIERS

♦ **Angel:** Jophiel
♦ **Chakra:** Third Eye
♦ **Crystals:** Agate, alexandrite, calcite, rose quartz
♦ **Tarot:** The Lovers
♦ **Sacred to:** Mabon

> **DIY TIP:** Hold a sprig of skullcap during meditation to ground you to the earth. Add skullcap to handfasting ceremonies to strengthen the lovers' oath.

FOR GARDENING

Skullcap is easy to grow; it will tolerate heat, drought, shade, and poor soil. It has few insect pests and rabbits, and deer won't eat it.

Suggested Varieties for Beginners: American skullcap

Location: USDA Plant Hardiness Zone 2–7

Light: Part shade to full sun

Water and Food: Regular watering, fertilize with a balanced fertilizer in early spring

Soil, Pot, Cultivation: Well-drained soil; grow in a 12-inch pot; propagate by root division, cuttings, or seeds

SNAPDRAGON

Antirrhinum

Size: 6 to 48 inches

Parts Used: Flowers, seeds

Safety Considerations: Nontoxic for humans and pets.

Planetary Ruler: Mars

Moon Phase: Full

Element: Fire

Zodiac Sign: Taurus

Gender: Masculine

Deity: Flora

Lore: The seedpods of snapdragons look like tiny shrunken skulls and have been the source of many legends; if a woman eats the pods, her beauty will be restored, whereas dried pods sprinkled around the house will bring protection from the spirit world.

Magical Purpose: Protection

MAGICAL AMPLIFIERS

- ◆ **Angel:** Michael
- ◆ **Chakra:** Solar Plexus
- ◆ **Crystals:** Agate, hematite, sardonyx
- ◆ **Tarot:** Strength

> **DIY TIP:** Snapdragons dislike summer heat and will stop blooming, but keep them well watered, and they'll flower again later in the season.

FOR GARDENING

Snapdragons are perennials usually grown as annuals; they are a much-loved classic cottage-garden flower.

Suggested Varieties for Beginners: Rocket, Madame Butterfly

Location: USDA Plant Hardiness Zone 7–11

Light: Full sun to part shade

Water and Food: Regular watering, fertilize when flowers appear

Soil, Pot, Cultivation: Rich, moist, well-drained soil; grow in 8-inch pots; pinch stem tips to encourage bushiness, deadhead spent flowers

SPIKENARD

Aralia racemosa

Size: 1 to 3 feet

Parts Used: Leaves, flowers, root, berries

Safety Considerations: Edible. Nontoxic for humans and pets.

Planetary Ruler: Venus

Moon Phase: Waxing

Element: Water

Zodiac Sign: Cancer

Gender: Feminine

Deity: Holda, Vesta

Lore: Spikenard is mentioned in the Bible as a plant used for its fragrance.

Magical Purpose: Fidelity, health

MAGICAL AMPLIFIERS

- **Angel:** Uriel
- **Chakra:** Crown
- **Crystals:** Amber, rose quartz, sodalite
- **Tarot:** The Lovers

DIY TIP: Mix dried spikenard with sandalwood essential oil and burn on a charcoal disc to promote a happy marriage.

FOR FORAGING

Spikenard has small edible berries that ripen in September, and the root and young leaves may be used in soups and stews. Spikenard root can be used as a substitute for ginseng because they are in the same family. Forage throughout North America. USDA Plant Hardiness Zone 4-8

SPURGE

Euphorbia

Size: 3 to 36 inches

Parts Used: Flowers, leaves

Safety Considerations: Toxic for humans and pets. All parts of spurge are toxic if ingested; always wear gloves when handling. All spurges exude a toxic white latex sap that is irritating to the skin.

Planetary Ruler: Saturn

Moon Phase: Waning

Element: Water

Zodiac Sign: Taurus

Gender: Feminine

Lore: In South Africa, spurge is called dead man's tree because of its toxic sap.

Magical Purpose: Purification, protection

MAGICAL AMPLIFIERS

- ♦ **Angel:** Gabriel
- ♦ **Chakra:** Solar Plexus
- ♦ **Crystals:** Selenite, howlite, quartz
- ♦ **Tarot:** The Star

> **DIY TIP:** Take cuttings in the spring and stop the latex from flowing by placing the cutting in cold water. Dust the cut surface with rooting hormone and place in a small pot filled with seed-starter soil.

FOR GARDENING

Spurge has more than 2,000 species, divided into succulents and perennials.

Suggested Varieties for Beginners: Cushion spurge, Blue Haze spurge

Location: USDA Plant Hardiness Zone 5–11

Light: Full sun

Water and Food: Regular watering, compost in spring, liquid fertilizer during the growing season

Soil, Pot, Cultivation: Sandy, well-drained soil; grow in 12-inch terra-cotta pots; propagate by stem cuttings

SQUILL
Scilla

Size: 4 to 8 inches

Parts Used: Flowers, leaves, bulbs

Safety Considerations: Poisonous to pets, toxic for humans. All parts of squill are toxic; always wear gloves when handling.

Planetary Ruler: Mars

Moon Phase: Waning

Element: Fire

Zodiac Sign: Leo

Gender: Masculine

Deity: Scylla

Lore: The name *Scilla* came from a Greek myth of a beautiful woman named Scylla who was transformed into a monster by the goddess Circe, who was jealous of her.

Magical Purpose: Money, protection, hex-breaking

MAGICAL AMPLIFIERS
- **Angel:** Michael
- **Chakra:** Solar Plexus
- **Crystals:** Amethyst, carnelian, fire opal
- **Tarot:** The Tower

DIY TIP: Naturalize squill under deciduous trees; they bloom very early and will finish blooming and disappear before the trees leaf out.

FOR GARDENING

Squill is a small plant with star- or bell-shaped flowers drooping on short stems. They're easy to grow and multiply through bulbs and reseeding.

Suggested Varieties for Beginner: Alpine squill

Location: USDA Plant Hardiness Zone 2–8

Light: Full sun to part shade

Water and Food: Light watering, drought tolerant once established, fertilize in spring with bulb fertilizer

Soil, Pot, Cultivation: Regular well-drained soil, grow in 6-inch pots, allow the foliage to dry naturally after blooming

ST. JOHN'S WORT

Hypericum perforatum

Size: 1 to 3 feet

Parts Used: Flowers

Safety Considerations: Toxic for humans and pets. All parts of St. John's wort are toxic if ingested in large amounts; always wear gloves when handling.

Planetary Ruler: Sun

Moon Phase: Waxing

Element: Fire

Zodiac Sign: Leo

Gender: Masculine

Deity: Baldur

Lore: Bringing St. John's wort flowers into the home on Midsummer Eve will bring protection from witches, the evil eye, and house fires.

Magical Purpose: Health, protection, strength

MAGICAL AMPLIFIERS

- **Angel:** Raphael
- **Chakra:** Third Eye
- **Crystals:** Amber, sunstone, topaz
- **Tarot:** The Sun
- **Sacred to:** Litha

FOR GARDENING

St. John's wort is an upright perennial plant with bright yellow flowers that bloom from June to September.

Suggested Varieties for Beginners:
Common St. John's wort

Location: USDA Plant Hardiness Zone 3–8

Light: Full sun to part shade

Water and Food: Regular watering, add compost in the spring

Soil, Pot, Cultivation: Rich, well-drained soil; grow in 12-inch pots; cut back in early spring

DIY TIP: Too much sun will cause leaf scorch, and too little sun will result in fewer flowers. The best location is one with morning sun and shade in the afternoon.

STRAWBERRY

Fragaria × ananassa

Size: 6 to 8 inches

Parts Used: Leaves, fruit

Safety Considerations: Edible. Nontoxic for humans and pets.

Planetary Ruler: Venus

Moon Phase: Full

Element: Water

Zodiac Sign: Libra

Gender: Feminine

Deity: Venus, Freya, Frigg

Lore: The red color and heart shape of strawberries make them sacred to love goddesses.

Magical Purpose: Love, luck, visions

MAGICAL AMPLIFIERS

- **Angel:** Gabriel
- **Chakra:** Sacral
- **Crystals:** Carnelian, lapis lazuli, topaz
- **Tarot:** The High Priest

DIY TIP: Double strawberries are potent love charms.

FOR GARDENING

Strawberries are delicate plants susceptible to root rot, mold, viruses, and pests. Mulch with straw, grass clippings, shredded leaves, or pine needles.

Suggested Varieties for Beginners: Primetime, Sable

Location: USDA Plant Hardiness Zone 5–8

Light: Full sun

Water and Food: Generous watering during fruit production, feed with compost or manure in the spring, feed again after fruiting with a balanced fertilizer

Soil, Pot, Cultivation: Loamy soil with added organic matter, grow in 8-inch pots, cut plants down to 1 inch in the fall

SUMMER SAVORY

Satureja hortensis

Size: 6 to 18 inches

Parts Used: Leaves

Safety Considerations: Edible. Nontoxic for humans and pets.

Planetary Ruler: Mercury

Moon Phase: New

Element: Air

Zodiac Sign: Gemini, Virgo

Gender: Masculine

Deity: Athena, Pan

Lore: Ancient Romans believed that savory was a natural aphrodisiac and used it in love potions. The Latin name for savory is *Satureja* or *Satyr*, a mythical being who loved women, drinking, and parties!

Magical Purpose: Mental powers, love

MAGICAL AMPLIFIERS

- ♦ **Angel:** Raphael
- ♦ **Chakra:** Throat
- ♦ **Crystals:** Sunstone, tiger's-eye
- ♦ **Tarot:** The Sun

> **DIY TIP:** Wear a crown of savory to help keep you awake. Burn dried savory to increase intellect and creativity.

FOR GARDENING

Summer savory is easy to grow in dryish soil but will need winter protection in cold areas. It's very attractive to bees and is deer resistant.

Suggested Varieties for Beginners: Summer savory

Location: USDA Plant Hardiness Zone 1–11

Light: Full sun

Water and Food: Regular watering, add compost in the summer

Soil, Pot, Cultivation: Average soil, grow in 12-inch pots, harvest just before flowering

SUNFLOWER

Helianthus annuus

Size: 6 to 14 feet

Parts Used: Seeds, petals

Safety Considerations: Edible. Nontoxic for humans and pets.

Planetary Ruler: Sun

Moon Phase: New

Element: Fire

Zodiac Sign: Leo

Gender: Masculine

Deity: Demeter, Modron, Apollo

Lore: Apollo turned his jealous lover Clytie into a sunflower, but she still adored him and turned her flower head to watch him move across the sky.

Magical Purpose: Cheerfulness, wishes, health, wisdom

MAGICAL AMPLIFIERS

- ◆ **Angel:** Michael
- ◆ **Chakra:** Solar Plexus
- ◆ **Crystals:** Peridot, turquoise
- ◆ **Tarot:** The Empress

DIY TIP: Dry whole sunflower heads and offer them as winter food for the birds.

FOR GARDENING

Sunflowers may need to be staked and are best planted in a sheltered location away from strong wind to protect heavy seed heads.

Suggested Varieties for Beginners: Evening Sun, Autumn Beauty

Location: USDA Plant Hardiness Zone 4–9; grow as an annual in cooler zones

Light: Full sun

Water and Food: Regular watering, feed regularly during the growing season

Soil, Pot, Cultivation: Loose, well-drained soil amended with compost; grow small varieties in deep pots; heat and drought tolerant

SWEET GUM

Liquidambar styraciflua

Size: 70 feet

Parts Used: Leaves, bark, fruit

Safety Considerations: Edible. Nontoxic for humans and pets.

Planetary Ruler: Sun

Moon Phase: Waning

Element: Fire

Zodiac Sign: Sagittarius

Gender: Masculine

Deity: Mithras

Lore: Sweet gum was introduced to European consciousness by a Spanish conquistador in 1519, when he witnessed a ceremony between Cortés and Montezuma in which sweet gum resin was used.

Magical Purpose: Protection

MAGICAL AMPLIFIERS

◆ **Angel:** Michael

◆ **Chakra:** Solar Plexus

◆ **Crystals:** Carnelian, red jasper, ruby

◆ **Tarot:** The Emperor

FOR FORAGING

Sweet gum is a deciduous tree common in the southeastern United States. Forage in the southeastern United States. USDA Plant Hardiness Zone 6–10

DIY TIP: Use a mulch of sweet gum "balls" around plants to deter snails. The tree bark is the source of the incense resin called storax.

SWEET PEA

Lathyrus odoratus

Size: 6 to 8 feet

Parts Used: Flowers

Safety Considerations: Toxic for humans and pets. Sweet pea seeds are mildly toxic if ingested, and the plants are safe to handle without gloves.

Planetary Ruler: Venus

Moon Phase: Waxing

Element: Water

Zodiac Sign: Virgo

Gender: Feminine

Lore: Sweet pea is a relatively young plant developed in England from seeds received from Italy by Henry Eckford. According to the language of flowers, *sweet pea* means "good wishes, friendship, and goodbyes."

Magical Purpose: Friendship, chastity

MAGICAL AMPLIFIERS

- ♦ **Angel:** Zadkiel
- ♦ **Chakra:** Third Eye
- ♦ **Crystals:** Moss agate, rose quartz, pink tourmaline
- ♦ **Tarot:** The Lovers

DIY TIP: Plant sweet peas in late winter or early spring and pinch back the growing tip when it's 4 inches tall to encourage branching.

FOR GARDENING

Sweet peas are climbing plants with clusters of sweetly scented flowers in many colors.

Suggested Varieties for Beginners: Old-Fashioned

Location: USDA Plant Hardiness Zone 3–8

Light: Full sun to part shade

Water and Food: Regular watering, high-potassium fertilizer monthly, bloodmeal when planting

Soil, Pot, Cultivation: Rich, well-drained soil; grow in 14-inch pots; cut spent blooms for continual flowers

SWEET WOODRUFF
Galium odoratum

Size: 6 to 12 inches

Parts Used: Stems, leaves, flowers

Safety Considerations: Nontoxic in small amounts for humans; nontoxic for pets.

Planetary Ruler: Mars

Moon Phase: Waxing

Element: Fire

Zodiac Sign: Aries

Gender: Masculine

Deity: Gaia

Lore: During the Middle Ages, woodruff was called "bedstraw" and was used as a sweet-smelling filling for mattresses. It is traditional to add sweet woodruff to Beltane "May Wine."

Magical Purpose: Victory, protection, money

MAGICAL AMPLIFIERS

- ◆ **Angel:** Michael
- ◆ **Chakra:** Solar Plexus
- ◆ **Crystals:** Aventurine, carnelian, unakite
- ◆ **Tarot:** The Chariot
- ◆ **Sacred to:** Beltane

FOR GARDENING

Sweet woodruff is a low creeping, aromatic perennial used as a flowering ground cover in shady areas.

Location: USDA Plant Hardiness Zone 4–8

Light: Part shade to full shade

Water and Food: Regular watering, fertilizer is not required

Soil, Pot, Cultivation: Rich, loamy, well-drained soil; grow in 12-inch pots; divide by digging up root sections and replanting

DIY TIP: Harvest the leaves after the plant blooms. Dry sweet woodruff to increase its aroma; when placed in sachets and potpourris, the scent can last for years.

SWEETGRASS

Hierochloe odorata

Size: 1 to 3 feet

Parts Used: Leaves

Safety Considerations: Nontoxic for humans and pets.

Planetary Ruler: Venus

Moon Phase: Waning

Element: Air

Zodiac Sign: Pisces

Gender: Feminine

Deity: Hecate

Lore: Sweetgrass is sacred to Indigenous Peoples, including the Kiowa, Cheyenne, Gros Ventre, and Lakota, and is used as a smudging herb during rituals.

Magical Purpose: Calling spirits, purification

MAGICAL AMPLIFIERS

- ◆ **Angel:** Gabriel
- ◆ **Chakra:** Crown
- ◆ **Crystals:** Fluorite, peridot, tiger's-eye
- ◆ **Tarot:** The Moon

FOR FORAGING

Sweetgrass has a beautiful vanilla-like scent once it is dried. Forage throughout North America. USDA Plant Hardiness Zone 3–8

DIY TIP: To braid sweetgrass, place the leaves in warm water for 15 minutes to make them more flexible. The three braided strands represent mind, body, and spirit.

TANSY

Tanacetum vulgare

Size: 2 to 3 feet

Parts Used: Flowers, leaves

Safety Considerations: Toxic for humans and pets.

Planetary Ruler: Venus

Moon Phase: Waxing

Element: Water

Zodiac Sign: Gemini

Gender: Feminine

Deity: Hebe, Ganymede

Lore: The Egyptians used tansy as an embalming herb and scattered it on floors to deter rodents and insects.

Magical Purpose: Health, longevity

MAGICAL AMPLIFIERS

- ◆ **Angel:** Raphael
- ◆ **Chakra:** Solar Plexus
- ◆ **Crystals:** Citrine, petrified wood, sunstone
- ◆ **Tarot:** Temperance

FOR FORAGING

Tansy can be invasive, and the scent deters insects and animals. It is considered a noxious weed in many states. All parts of tansy are toxic if ingested but are safe to handle. Forage throughout North America. USDA Plant Hardiness Zone 4–8

DIY TIP: Cut tansy down to the ground as soon as flowers appear to prevent it from going to seed and taking over your garden. Hang plants upside down to dry.

THISTLE

Cirsium

Size: 2 to 3 feet

Parts Used: Flowers, leaves, stalks

Safety Considerations: Nontoxic for humans and pets.

Planetary Ruler: Mars

Moon Phase: Waxing

Element: Fire

Zodiac Sign: Scorpio

Gender: Masculine

Deity: Minerva, Thor

Lore: Thistle is the symbol of Scotland, and legend has it that sleeping Scots warriors were saved when an ambushing party of Norsemen stepped on thistle plants and screamed out in pain.

Magical Purpose: Endurance, unity, victory

MAGICAL AMPLIFIERS

- ◆ **Angel:** Chamuel
- ◆ **Chakra:** Root
- ◆ **Crystals:** Alexandrite, fluorite
- ◆ **Tarot:** The Devil
- ◆ **Sacred to:** Mabon

DIY TIP: Place a vase of thistle flowers nearby for renewed strength and vitality. Add thistle leaves to spell jars for added protection.

FOR FORAGING

Thistle leaves, stems, and flowers are edible, but thistle flowers may cause digestive issues, so be cautious. Forage throughout North America. USDA Plant Hardiness Zone 5–9

THYME

Thymus vulgaris

Size: 6 to 12 inches

Parts Used: Leaves

Safety Considerations: Edible. Nontoxic for humans and pets.

Planetary Ruler: Venus

Moon Phase: New

Element: Water

Zodiac Sign: Aries, Capricorn, Libra, Taurus

Gender: Feminine

Deity: Freya, Aphrodite, Ares

Lore: Fairies love thyme, and it's believed they gather at midsummer to dance upon it.

Magical Purpose: Honesty, healing, strength, purification

MAGICAL AMPLIFIERS

- **Angel:** Gabriel
- **Chakra:** Throat
- **Crystals:** Bloodstone, cat's-eye, jasper
- **Tarot:** The Hermit
- **Sacred to:** Summer Solstice

▌ **DIY TIP:** Burn thyme to repel insects.

FOR GARDENING

Thyme makes an excellent container plant and is pest- and disease-free. Cut back in early spring to stimulate new growth.

Suggested Varieties for Beginners: French or English thyme

Location: USDA Plant Hardiness Zone 5–7

Light: Full sun

Water and Food: Water when soil is dry, add compost in the spring, divide 4-year-old plants

Soil, Pot, Cultivation: Average soil, grow in 8-inch clay pots with good drainage, cut back after flowering

TULIP
Tulipa

Size: 9 to 24 inches

Parts Used: Flower

Safety Considerations: Edible. Toxic to pets. Bulbs toxic to humans, whereas flowers are nontoxic.

Planetary Ruler: Venus

Moon Phase: Full

Element: Earth

Zodiac Sign: Virgo

Gender: Feminine

Deity: Flora

Lore: Tulip was likely one of the first flowers grown simply for its beauty. Images of tulips have been found on pottery that dates to 2200 BCE.

Magical Purpose: Prosperity, love, protection

MAGICAL AMPLIFIERS

- **Angel:** Chamuel
- **Chakra:** Heart
- **Crystals:** Emerald, rose quartz, lapis lazuli
- **Tarot:** The Empress

DIY TIP: Plant the bulbs with the pointy end facing up, 4 to 8 inches deep in the fall. Bulbs should be spaced 2 to 5 inches apart.

FOR GARDENING

Tulips have been cultivated and hybridized to produce every color except blue.

Suggested Varieties for Beginners: Darwin Hybrid

Location: USDA Plant Hardiness Zone 3–8

Light: Full sun

Water and Food: Regular watering, add bulb food when planting, feed again in the spring

Soil, Pot, Cultivation: Rich, well-drained soil; grow in 12-inch pots; cut back flowers after blooming

UVA URSI
Arctostaphylos uva-ursi

Size: 2 to 12 inches

Parts Used: Leaves, flowers, branches

Safety Considerations: Edible. In small amounts, nontoxic for humans and pets.

Planetary Ruler: Saturn

Moon Phase: Full

Element: Earth

Zodiac Sign: Scorpio

Gender: Feminine

Deity: Cronus, Saturn

Lore: Marco Polo reported in the thirteenth century that uva ursi was being used by the Chinese to treat kidney and urinary issues.

Magical Purpose: Enhance psychic ability

MAGICAL AMPLIFIERS
- **Angel:** Gabriel
- **Chakra:** Third Eye
- **Crystals:** Amethyst, angelite, opal
- **Tarot:** The Hermit

FOR FORAGING

The berries are best if cooked and taste somewhat like cranberries. A tea made with fresh leaves can help treat infections and kidney issues. Forage throughout North America. USDA Plant Hardiness Zone 2–6

DIY TIP: Infuse uva ursi in warm water to make a potion used to cleanse talismans.

VALERIAN

Valeriana officinalis

Size: 1 to 4 feet

Parts Used: Flowers, leaves, root

Safety Considerations: Edible. Nontoxic for humans and pets.

Planetary Ruler: Venus, Mercury

Moon Phase: Full

Element: Water

Zodiac Sign: Scorpio, Virgo

Gender: Feminine

Deity: Epona

Lore: Dioscorides, a Roman physician from the first century, called it "Phu" because the roots smell awful.

Magical Purpose: Sleep, healing, longevity, romance, truth

MAGICAL AMPLIFIERS

♦ **Angel:** Raphael
♦ **Chakras:** Root, Throat
♦ **Crystals:** Amethyst, jasper, pyrite
♦ **Tarot:** Temperance

DIY TIP: Dig the roots in the fall and dry them in an out-of-the-way place to avoid the bad smell.

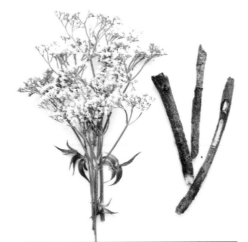

FOR GARDENING

Valerian blooms from early summer to fall; the flowers are fragrant and attractive to butterflies and birds.

Suggested Varieties for Beginners: Common valerian

Location: USDA Plant Hardiness Zone 4–9

Light: Full sun to part shade

Water and Food: Regular to generous watering; add compost in the spring

Soil, Pot, Cultivation: Moist soil; grow in 12-inch pots; will self-seed, can be invasive

VERVAIN
Verbena officinalis

Size: 12 to 36 inches

Parts Used: Leaves, stems, flowers

Safety Considerations: For humans, nontoxic in small amounts; for pets, toxic.

Planetary Ruler: Venus

Moon Phase: New

Element: Earth, Air, Fire

Zodiac Sign: Capricorn, Gemini, Sagittarius

Gender: Feminine

Deity: Cerridwen, Diana, Hermes, Isis, Thor

Lore: During the Middle Ages, vervain was called the magician's herb, and it has always been associated with magic and witchcraft.

Magical Purpose: Love, protection, purification, peace, sleep, healing

MAGICAL AMPLIFIERS

- ◆ **Angel:** Chamuel
- ◆ **Chakra:** Root
- ◆ **Crystals:** Lapis lazuli
- ◆ **Tarot:** The Magician
- ◆ **Sacred to:** Litha

> **DIY TIP:** Gather vervain before dawn on the first day of the New Moon for the highest magical potency.

FOR GARDENING

Vervain is a fast-growing herb that is drought tolerant; it has spikes of tiny flowers that bloom from early summer to fall.

Suggested Varieties for Beginners: Common vervain

Location: USDA Plant Hardiness Zone 4–8

Light: Full sun

Water and Food: Light watering after the plant is established, add compost in the spring

Soil, Pot, Cultivation: Regular well-drained soil, grow in 12-inch pots, cut back in the middle of the growing season

WHITE OAK

Quercus alba

Size: 5 to 80 feet

Parts Used: Leaves, bark, twigs, acorns

Safety Considerations: Edible. Nontoxic for humans and pets.

Planetary Ruler: Sun

Moon Phase: Waning

Element: Fire

Zodiac Sign: Sagittarius

Gender: Masculine

Deity: Dagda, Hecate, Pan

Lore: In fairy lore, oak, ash, and thorn are the three primary magical trees that were portals to other realms.

Magical Purpose: Protection, health, money, fertility, luck

MAGICAL AMPLIFIERS

- ◆ **Angel:** Michael
- ◆ **Chakra:** Root
- ◆ **Crystals:** Obsidian, pyrite, tourmaline
- ◆ **Tarot:** The Emperor

FOR FORAGING

Remove tannic acid from acorns before eating by boiling the shelled nuts in water for 15 minutes. Discard the discolored water, add fresh water, and repeat the boiling process several times. Forage throughout North America. USDA Plant Hardiness Zone 5–9

DIY TIP: For courage, surround a golden candle with oak leaves, light it, and meditate on your goal.

WILD GERANIUM

Geranium maculatum

Size: 18 to 24 inches

Parts Used: Leaves, flowers

Safety Considerations: Edible. Nontoxic for humans and pets.

Planetary Ruler: Venus

Moon Phase: Full

Element: Water

Zodiac Sign: Cancer

Gender: Feminine

Deity: Kuan Yin

Lore: Wild geranium contains tannin, used by American colonists to tan hides.

Magical Purpose: Fertility, love, protection

MAGICAL AMPLIFIERS

♦ **Angel:** Chamuel

♦ **Chakra:** Root

♦ **Crystals:** Amazonite, jade, moss agate

♦ **Tarot:** The Emperor

DIY TIP: You can easily root wild geranium in water. Cut the stem with a sharp knife just below a leaf node, trim all the leaves except the top two, and place them in a water-filled vase.

FOR FORAGING

Wild geranium roots and leaves can be made into a tea to treat sore throats and prevent constipation. Forage throughout the Midwest, Northeast, and western United States. USDA Plant Hardiness Zone 5–8

WILD GINGER

Asarum canadense, caudatum

Size: 3 to 5 inches

Parts Used: Leaves, root

Safety Considerations: Edible. Mildly toxic to humans; toxic for pets.

Planetary Ruler: Moon

Moon Phase: Full

Element: Water

Zodiac Sign: Cancer

Gender: Feminine

Deity: Artemis, Flora, Maia

Lore: Early European colonizers used wild ginger to replace Asian ginger and made tea from candied roots.

Magical Purpose: Love, passion, fertility

MAGICAL AMPLIFIERS

- ◆ **Angel:** Chamuel
- ◆ **Chakra:** Heart
- ◆ **Crystals:** Amethyst, lepidolite, sardonyx
- ◆ **Tarot:** The Lovers

FOR FORAGING

The root has a strong ginger flavor and is safe to eat in small amounts. Forage throughout North America. USDA Plant Hardiness Zone 3–7

DIY TIP: Wild ginger makes a beautiful ground cover for shady spots and is deer resistant.

WILD TOBACCO

Nicotiana rustica

Size: 3 to 6 feet

Parts Used: Leaves

Safety Considerations: Poisonous to humans and pets. All parts are deadly poison if ingested; always wear gloves when handling.

Planetary Ruler: Mars

Moon Phase: Full

Element: Fire

Zodiac Sign: Sagittarius

Gender: Masculine

Deity: Tezcatlipoca

Lore: Sharing tobacco smoke is sacred to Indigenous Peoples such as the Nez Perce and Inuit.

Magical Purpose: Healing, offerings, purification

MAGICAL AMPLIFIERS

- ◆ **Angel:** Raphael
- ◆ **Chakra:** Heart
- ◆ **Crystals:** Amber, jasper, moss agate
- ◆ **Tarot:** The Sun

> **DIY TIP:** Dry tobacco leaves in the fall once they have turned yellow. Hang in bunches of three to five leaves in a shed or garage away from direct sunlight. Wild tobacco is toxic and is for ritual use only.

FOR GARDENING

Wild tobacco is an annual wildflower native to North America and is a nightshade.

Location: USDA Plant Hardiness Zone 7–10

Light: Full sun

Water and Food: Generous watering, add tomato fertilizer monthly until flowers appear

Soil, Pot, Cultivation: Regular well-drained soil, grow in 18-inch pots, pinch out the plants as soon as they flower

WILD VIOLET

Viola sororia

Size: 4 to 10 inches

Parts Used: Flowers, leaves

Safety Considerations: Edible. Nontoxic for humans and pets.

Planetary Ruler: Venus

Moon Phase: Waxing

Element: Water

Zodiac Sign: Scorpio

Gender: Feminine

Deity: Aphrodite, Priapus

Lore: During the Middle Ages, people believed that violet flowers bowed their heads in sorrow after the crucifixion.

Magical Purpose: Protection, luck, lust, wishes, healing

MAGICAL AMPLIFIERS

- **Angel:** Jophiel
- **Chakra:** Third Eye
- **Crystals:** Amethyst, lepidolite, kunzite
- **Tarot:** The Star
- **Sacred to:** Ostara

FOR FORAGING

Violet leaves are a great addition to salads, and the flowers have a soft, sweet floral taste. The flowers may also be made into jam, jelly, or syrup. Forage throughout North America. USDA Plant Hardiness Zone 3–8

DIY TIP: Steep violet flowers in hot water to make a tea that will alleviate heartbreak. Dreaming of violets is a sign that money is coming to you.

WILLOW

Salix

Size: 2 to 50 feet

Parts Used: Leaves, stems, branches, bark

Safety Considerations: Edible. Nontoxic for humans and pets.

Planetary Ruler: Moon

Moon Phase: Full

Element: Water

Zodiac Sign: Pisces

Gender: Feminine

Deity: Hecate, Persephone, The Morrigan

Lore: In Druid lore, the universe hatched from two scarlet eggs nested in a willow tree: one egg was the Sun, and the other was the Earth.

Magical Purpose: Enchantment, witchcraft, immortality

MAGICAL AMPLIFIERS

- **Angel:** Azrael
- **Chakra:** Heart
- **Crystals:** Carnelian, moonstone, lepidolite
- **Tarot:** Death
- **Sacred to:** Beltane

FOR FORAGING

The inner bark contains salicylic acid, a forerunner of aspirin, and is used for pain relief. Forage throughout North America. USDA Plant Hardiness Zone 3–9

DIY TIP: With permission, cut a willow wand to use for Moon magic, for protection, and to aid you with meditative journeys to the Underworld.

WITCH HAZEL

Hamamelis

Size: 10 to 20 feet

Parts Used: Flowers, leaves, bark

Safety Considerations: Toxic to pets, nontoxic for humans.

Planetary Ruler: Saturn

Moon Phase: Waning

Element: Fire

Zodiac Sign: Capricorn

Gender: Masculine

Lore: Witch hazel branches are used for dowsing, or "water-witching," and it's said that the branch will become "lively" when it detects water.

Magical Purpose: Protection, chastity

MAGICAL AMPLIFIERS

- ◆ **Angel:** Uriel
- ◆ **Chakra:** Solar Plexus
- ◆ **Crystals:** Agate, diamond, onyx
- ◆ **Tarot:** The Magician
- ◆ **Sacred to:** Samhain

> **DIY TIP:** Make a witch hazel decoction by boiling half a pound of witch hazel twigs in a gallon of water for about 30 minutes.

FOR GARDENING

Witch Hazel is a shrub with bright yellow flowers that bloom in the fall or late winter, depending on the variety.

Suggested Varieties for Beginners: American or common witch hazel

Location: USDA Plant Hardiness Zone 3–9

Light: Full sun

Water and Food: Regular watering, liquid fertilizer monthly during the growing season

Soil, Pot, Cultivation: Loamy, moist, well-drained soil; not suitable for pots, grow in-ground; pruning is not required

WOOD SORREL

Oxalis acetosella

Size: 6 to 10 inches

Parts Used: Leaves, flowers

Safety Considerations: Edible. For humans, nontoxic in small amounts; for pets, toxic. Those who are pregnant and people with gout should avoid consuming it.

Planetary Ruler: Venus

Moon Phase: Waxing

Element: Earth

Zodiac Sign: Virgo

Gender: Feminine

Deity: Triple Goddess

Lore: The Celts associated wood sorrel with leprechauns, and there's a theory that the Irish shamrock was originally a wood sorrel.

Magical Purpose: Healing

MAGICAL AMPLIFIERS

- ◆ **Angel:** Raphael
- ◆ **Chakra:** Solar Plexus
- ◆ **Crystals:** Clear quartz, obsidian, rose quartz
- ◆ **Tarot:** The Star
- ◆ **Sacred to:** Litha

FOR FORAGING

Wood sorrel is high in vitamin C and tastes tart and lemony, though it may cause kidney stones. Forage throughout North America. USDA Plant Hardiness Zone 5–11

DIY TIP: Dry sorrel leaves and use them in fairy magic, healing magic, and rituals.

THE GREEN WITCH'S HERB AND PLANT ENCYCLOPEDIA

WORMWOOD

Artemisia absinthium

Size: 1 to 5 feet

Parts Used: Leaves, flowers, stems

Safety Considerations: Toxic for humans and pets. All parts are toxic if ingested; always wear gloves when handling.

Planetary Ruler: Mars, Saturn

Moon Phase: Full

Element: Earth

Zodiac Sign: Gemini

Gender: Masculine

Deity: Diana, Artemis, Hecate

Lore: Wormwood is the main ingredient in absinthe, the alcoholic beverage said to produce vision, summon spirits, and cause madness. Witches planted wormwood in their gardens to prevent poisoning when working with toxic plants.

Magical Purpose: Astral travel, binding, clairvoyance

MAGICAL AMPLIFIERS

♦ **Angel:** Gabriel
♦ **Chakra:** Root
♦ **Crystals:** Amethyst, selenite, sodalite
♦ **Tarot:** The Tower
♦ **Sacred to:** Samhain

> **DIY TIP:** Rub fresh wormwood leaves on magical tools to be used in spirit work to repel baneful energy and connect the tools with the otherworld.

FOR GARDENING

Wormwood is a low-maintenance perennial herb with lacy, olive-green aromatic foliage.

Suggested Varieties for Beginners: Common wormwood

Location: USDA Plant Hardiness Zone 3-10

Light: Full sun

Water and Food: Light watering, fertilizer not required, add compost in spring

Soil, Pot, Cultivation: Average, well-drained soil; grow in 14-inch pots; divide the plant when it outgrows the pot

YARROW

Achillea millefolium

Size: 2 to 3 feet

Parts Used: Leaves, flowers, root

Safety Considerations: Edible. Mildly toxic to humans; toxic for pets.

Planetary Ruler: Venus

Moon Phase: Waxing

Element: Water

Zodiac Sign: Gemini

Gender: Feminine

Deity: Cernunnos

Lore: Yarrow's botanical name *Achillea* derives from the mythical Greek Achilles, and yarrow was used to heal battle wounds. This medicinal property is reflected in some of yarrow's common names: staunchweed and soldier's woundwort.

Magical Purpose: Courage, psychic powers, exorcism

MAGICAL AMPLIFIERS

- **Angel:** Michael
- **Chakra:** Root
- **Crystals:** Peridot, shungite, smoky quartz
- **Tarot:** The High Priestess

FOR FORAGING

Yarrow leaves are edible but have a bitter taste. The flowers can be used as a substitute for hops in home brewing. Forage throughout North America. USDA Plant Hardiness Zone 3–9

DIY TIP: Add a sprig of yarrow to any floral bouquet to dispel negative energy, sorrow, or depression. Keep some dried yarrow flowers with your tarot cards or divination tools to boost their receptivity.

YEW

Taxus baccata

Size: 4 to 20 feet

Parts Used: Leaves, bark, twigs, berries

Safety Considerations: Poisonous to humans and pets. All parts are deadly poison if ingested; always wear gloves when handling.

Planetary Ruler: Saturn, Pluto

Moon Phase: New

Element: Water

Zodiac Sign: Scorpio

Gender: Feminine

Deity: Artemis, Astarte, Hecate

Lore: An ancient Norse belief was that the yew stood between the worlds of living and death and could trap wandering spirits within its branches.

Magical Purpose: Spirit communication

MAGICAL AMPLIFIERS

- **Angel:** Azrael
- **Chakra:** Root
- **Crystal:** Olivine
- **Tarot:** Death
- **Sacred to:** Samhain, Yule

FOR FORAGING

Yew is considered one of the most poisonous trees in the world. Forage throughout North America. USDA Plant Hardiness Zone 2–10

DIY TIP: To make powerful runes and ogham staves, carve them from yew wood, but be careful not to breathe the toxic dust.

DIRECTORY OF HERBS BY NEED

RESOURCES

✦ Books

Complete Book of Correspondences by Sandra Kynes is a complete magical correspondence reference book invaluable for casting and creating rituals.

Encyclopedia of Magical Herbs by Scott Cunningham is a classic herbal reference book that should be in every witch's library.

Foraging: A Beginner's Guide for Foragers by Andrew Robinson is a great beginner's book for wild foraging.

Green Witchcraft by Paige Vanderbeck is a practical guide to the magic of plants, herbs, crystals, and more.

The Green Witchcraft Bible by Sheila Paltrow includes healing and natural magic by mastering herbs, essential oils, and flowers.

Herb Magic by Patti Wigington is a guide to magical herbalism that introduces the spiritual side of herbs and how to use them.

The Master Book of Herbalism by Paul Beyerl is a complete herbal reference that includes medicinal, magical, and religious use of herbs.

Rodale's Ultimate Encyclopedia of Organic Gardening by Deborah L. Martin, Fern Marshall Bradley, Barbara W. Ellis, and Ellen Phillips is a practical handbook filled with easy-to-follow information collected from experts.

Wildcrafting Weeds by Colleen Codekas and Joel Schwartz has information on 20 common edible and medicinal plants growing in your backyard.

✦ Online Resources

Alchemy-Works.com is a reliable source for hard-to-get seeds and a wealth of magic information.

Almanac.com is the Farmer's Almanac website with everything you need to know to plant, grow, and harvest.

ASPCA.org/pet-care/animal-poison-control provides a plant toxicity guide for pets.

Botanical.com is my go-to site for everything herbal.

Gardenia.net provides garden design and plant care guides.

PoisonousPlants.ansci.cornell.edu is a resource listing plants poisonous to livestock and other animals.

TheHerbalAcademy.com has affordable herbal courses and a lot of free information.

TheSpruce.com is a home improvement site with an excellent garden plant section.

Witchipedia.com is a wiki for witches.

INDEX

✦ About the Author

Rowan Morgana is well known online through her websites at SacredWicca.com, MorganaMagickSpell.com, and Etsy shop Morgana Magick Spell and on social media. She has two previous books, *Modern Wicca* and *The Solitary Wicca Guide*. Besides honoring the seasonal changes with her Coven sisters, Rowan loves to be out in her large garden or camping with her husband.